MARCO POLO

G000081055

BRUGES, GHENT & ANTWERP

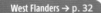

SYMBOLS

INSIDER TIP   Insider Tip

★   Highlight

●●●●   Best of ...

↙   Scenic view

☺   Responsible travel: fair
              trade principles and the
              environment respected

(*)   Telephone numbers
              that are not toll-free

PRICE CATEGORIES HOTELS

Expensive	over 140 euros
Moderate	90 – 140 euros
Budget	under 90 euros

Prices are for a double room
with breakfast

PRICE CATEGORIES RESTAURANTS

Expensive	over 50 euros
Moderate	30 – 50 euros
Budget	under 30 euros

Prices are for a three-course
meal excluding drinks

On the cover: Modern Museum in Antwerp -> p. 72 | Beer brewed in Watou -> p. 97

CONTENTS

Flemish Brabant → p. 58

Antwerp → p. 68

Limburg → p. 84

Road atlas → p. 122

DID YOU KNOW?
Timeline → p. 12
Urban gardening → p. 23
Local specialities → p. 26
Books & Films → p. 46
Veggiedag Ghent → p. 54
Lambic, Gueuze and Kriek → p. 62
Antwerp personal shopper → p. 74
Budgeting → p. 111
Weather in Oostende → p. 112

MAPS IN THE GUIDEBOOK
(124 A1) Page numbers and coordinates refer to the road atlas
(0) Site/address located off the map.
Coordinates are also given for places that are not marked on the road atlas

INSIDE BACK COVER:
PULL-OUT MAP →

PULL-OUT MAP 𝄜
(𝄜 A–B 2–3) Refers to the removable pull-out map

The best MARCO POLO Insider Tips

Our top 15 Insider Tips

INSIDERTIP Land of plenty

In Bruges, you can watch Juliette's team bake unusual organic spekulatius (spicy almond cookies) and gingerbread specialities → p. 37

INSIDERTIP Cool night

On the edge of Kortrijk, the chic D-Hotel boasts a spa that befits the region's true design capital → p. 42

INSIDERTIP Eco fashion

Antwerp's fashion designer Bruno Pieters only uses fabrics from organic agriculture and processed according to the principles of fair trade → p. 29

INSIDERTIP Fries galore

In Bruges' Frietmuseum the humble potato and fries take centre stage. It goes without saying that any visit has to culminate in a decent tasting → p. 34

INSIDERTIP Swinging nightlife

In the saloon-style bar Jigger's in Ghent, Olivier Jacobs mixes cocktails that have won several awards; some of them use the local genever - juniper spirit → p. 56

INSIDERTIP Veggie snack

At Snack Aahaar, Antwerp-based Indians prepare a varied vegetarian buffet – all you can eat for 9 euros → p. 76

INSIDERTIP Beers by the dozen

In the tranquil western Flemish artists' village of Watou, over a dozen hand-crafted tasty beers are served in the friendly taverns on the square → p. 97

INSIDERTIP Rococo and garden art

A festival for plants: the masters of Hex Castle cultivate magnificent roses and old varieties of vegetables (photo right) → p. 94

INSIDER TIP **Secret recipe**

Ghent-based Gruut microbrewery flavour their beer not with hops but with a secret spice mix – try the result at home and on the terrace → p. 54

INSIDER TIP **Nuit blanche**

The White Hotel offers top design in cool white in a trendy neighbourhood of Brussels. An excellent and practical touch are the scooters the hotel makes available to its guests → p. 63

INSIDER TIP **The sky is the limit**

Take off in style on the beach of Oostduinkerke: the new trendy sport of kitesurfing will take you from the sea into the air and back – pick up the basics at one of the local kitesurfing schools → p. 101

INSIDER TIP **Glittering light on the water:**

In Antwerp, romantic candlelight cruises pass through the brightly illuminated harbour → p. 71

INSIDER TIP **Biodivercity**

The 'BiodiverCity' section in the Musée des Sciences Naturelles in Brussels gives playful explanations for the often astonishing interaction of flora, fauna and humans in a major city. Children and adults too can check their own track record on the computer → p. 104

INSIDER TIP **Rocked to sleep**

The Andromeda eco hostel, a barge converted according to the latest ecological findings and moored off the beaten track in a canal, shows a different aspect of the city of Ghent → p. 56

INSIDER TIP **Trendy island**

The old port of Antwerp might be rough, but it's ideal for partying and strolling. More and more trendy eateries are opening up here, and an increasing number of star architects are designing fabulous and impressive buildings: 't Eilandje (photo left) → p. 71

BEST OF ...

FOR FREE

● *Panoramic views from the MAS*
In Antwerp's *MAS* (Museum aan de Stroom), handy escalators lead up ten floors inside the building, providing ever-changing views of the city, the harbour and the surrounding countryside. This moving boulevard is accessible up to midnight, for free → p. 72

● *Art and nature*
On the edge of Antwerp, the *Middelheimmuseum* has an impressive collection of sculptures by renowned sculptors post-Auguste Rodin. The temporary exhibitions taking place outdoors and in the pavilions are also free of charge (photo) → p. 73

● *Jingle bells*
The tower of the *Sint-Romboutskathedraal* has not one but two carillons, and on summer nights they are used for concerts. After all, Mechelen is home to the renowned carillon academy. Chairs are provided for free by the arts centre → p. 82

● *A glimpse of royal rooms*
When Belgium's king is on his summer holidays, his official residence, the *Palais du Roi*, may be visited – for free! The icing on the cake is the hall of mirrors with a ceiling decorated by avant-garde artist Jan Fabre using the shimmering carapaces of millions of beetles → p. 61

● *City festival in Ghent*
Ten days and ten nights, a wealth of free events at the *Gentse Feesten* draw music fans, theatre buffs and lovers of street performance into this student city. When night falls a fairy-tale light show is put on as a bonus → p. 106

● *Revealed: the secrets of the national park*
Flanders' only national park, *Hoge Kempen* in Limburg, boasts plenty of natural beauty in heather, forests and replanted wasteland. Free guided tours reveal all you need to know about the park's flora and fauna, rocks and history → p. 89

●●●● Dots in guidebook refer to 'Best of ...' tips

● *Honouring the fallen*
The walls of the *Menenpoort* in Ypres bear the names of nearly 55,000 dead of the First World War, whose remains were never found. Every evening at 8pm sharp, the firefighters' band honours all victims of war by playing the Last Post → p. 42

● *Fishing from the saddle*
Oostduinkerke is the last place where you can experience this: fishermen riding their heavy draught horses into the sea (photo) whatever the weather. The small grey crabs they net are turned into typically Flemish delicacies, fresh from the horse as it were. Background information is available at the local *Nationaal Visserijmuseum* → p. 46

● *Historic musical interpretation*
Flemish musicians such Philippe Herreweghe, the Kuijken Brothers and Paul van Nevel count amongst the pioneers of the authentic interpretation of sounds from polyphony to Baroque. Antwerp's music centre *AMUZ*, which used to put on exclusively period concerts, has now branched out to include works of the 19th and early 20th century → p. 78

● *Local flower power*
For over two centuries, the *Floralien* in Ghent have put on a unique show of the region's best flower growers and flower arrangers. Aficionados keep a keen eye out for their internationally renowned plants: azaleas and begonias → p. 106

● *National sport*
The (in)famous Ronde van Vlaanderen cycle race takes place on a single day, but all year round, fans can visit the *Centrum Ronde van Vlaanderen* to find out about the different stages of this popular sports event and the lives of its folk heroes → p. 57

● *Living nativity scenes*
The Kempenland region around Turnhout has held on to one of the most beautiful and authentic Christmas traditions. Traditional mangers are erected on the village squares, with life-size dolls illustrating the birth of Christ. The real attraction however are the cows, sheep, goats and chickens → p. 107

ONLY IN

BEST OF ...

AND IF IT RAINS?
Activities to brighten your day

● **Royal Belle Époque**
Leopold II had the *Koninklijke Gaandereien* built in Oostende, arcades measuring 400 m/over 1300 feet. Today, they are a place for a pleasant stroll on a rainy day, enjoying views of the beach and sea, and taking tea at the Thermae Palace Hotel → p. 44

● **Chocolate fun**
At the *Choco Center*, attached to the Choco Story chocolate museum in Bruges, you can watch chocolates and truffles being made – or even take part in a course to learn all the tricks of the trade → p. 99

● **Tropical vegetation**
The main attraction of Belgium's National Botanic Gardens is the *Palais des Plantes*, allowing visitors to get to know 18,000 plant species in gigantic glasshouses. The flora of Central Africa takes centre stage (photo) → p. 64

● **Art galore**
The *Musées Royaux des Beaux-Arts de Belgique* in Brussels form the largest museum complex in the country. If you continue to the Musée Magritte next door, take a break in the café and browse the shop, a rainy day passes in a jiffy → p. 61

● **Pool with a view**
The *spa at Hotel La Réserve* in Knokke is located on the 6th floor. Large glass panels allow for views of the sea and sky from the blue pool. This view alone magically produces relaxation even on grey rainy days → p. 41

● **Fine winged altar**
The *Ghent Altar* by brothers Hubert and Jan van Eyck in the Sint-Baafskathedraal is one of the highlights of European art. Take your time and delve into the countless details for fascinating discoveries → p. 52

RAIN

RELAX AND CHILL OUT
Take it easy and spoil yourself

● *Quiet Bruges*
Away from the tourist masses treading the cobblestones, the magnificent quiet garden of the *Sint-Sebastiaansgilde* makes an inviting place to catch your breath. Only the bells in the Renaissance tower serve as a reminder of time passing → **p. 35**

● *Bucolic pleasures*
In the rural restaurant *In de Wulf* on the border between Flanders and France diners can enjoy fascinating titbits prepared from seasonal local produce – best followed by a tranquil night in rooms without TV or Wi-Fi → **p. 97**

● *Cruisin' café*
Like the prow of a luxury liner, the snow-white café restaurant *Zuiderterras* rises above the Schelde river in Antwerp. The view glides far across the broad stream, where barges and yachts pass, and a glass of beer or wine creates a holiday mood (photo) → **p. 77**

● *Top terrace view*
Brussels hip eatery *Kwint* affords views – best enjoyed from the spacious terrace – of the magnificent axis leading from the Place Royale via the hanging gardens at your feet to the city hall tower and further into the Brabant landscape → **p. 61**

● *Rural idyll*
In the shadow of Ghent's *Sint-Pietersabdij* and above an arm of the river Schelde, discover a picturesque oasis of tranquillity: a meadow full of gnarled apple trees, an aromatic herb garden and even a veritable vineyard → **p. 52**

● *Aromatherapy*
The hotel's location on the edge of the national park and the fact that it boasts its own park would be enough to draw holidaymakers to the *La Butte aux Bois* hotel in Lanaken. The aroma & colour therapy in the in-house spa tops it all, however; in summer you're surrounded by flowers and shrubs in bloom and twittering birds in soft air → **p. 89**

INTRODUCTION

DISCOVER FLANDERS!

Flanders. The name alone of Belgium's northernmost region evokes distinct associations: towns with magnificent city halls and imposing bell towers – the belfries, or *belforts* in Flemish – tranquil beguine courts and lively market squares. Museums full of masterpieces by artists such as Hans Memling, Hubert and Jan van Eyck, Peter Paul Rubens and Anthony van Dyck. A coastline with hospitality that makes up for the sometimes miserable weather. Add to the mix a near-Mediterranean joie de vivre that finds expression in colourful processions, boisterous festivals and culinary treats. Take a closer look and you will discover contrasts: between cities and landscapes, the old and the new. The mere concept of 'Flanders' is slightly misleading, and only took root in the 19th century to describe the entire region. Historically the term comprises part of the old duchy of Flanders in the west, a piece of the former duchy of Brabant in the middle and a patchwork of the former duchies of Liège, Limburg and Loon in the east. Despite this, wealthy citizens everywhere wrested extensive liberties for their powerful cities from the nobility. What has remained is an eminently local perspective

Photo: Windmill on the canal near Damme

North Sea idyll with stripes: a clear summer day on the sandy beach of De Haan

on life. For all the Levantine diamond traders in Antwerp, masses of tourists in Bruges, and students from all over the world in Leuven, or Louvain –Flemings are *honkvast,* children of their town or village. Rarely will they move house, often commuting between their place of residence and a faraway workplace. A range of different linguistic idiosyncrasies is part of this local feeling. The nasal sounds of an Antwerp *sinjoor* announcing that his *metropool* is the navel of the world. The legendary tight-fistedness of the western Flemings is matched by their taciturnity and clipped, guttural sounds. The tradition of rebellious workers is reflected in the *gentenaars'* sharp, metallic way of talking, while the Limburgers have a broad, soft and slightly singing speech, a wonderful match for their *vlaaikes* fruit and jam cakes.

Local patriotism and Limburg fruit flan

Most Flemish people have an ambivalent attitude to landscape and nature. They insist on living surrounded by green spaces, yet few will tolerate trees in their gardens. That some 100 hectares of their already sparse woodland (150,000 hectares or 11

862 The duchy of Flanders emerges (becoming a French fiefdom in 1056)

1106 The dukes of Leuven become the dukes of Brabant (a German fiefdom)

1390 Brabant passes to the duchy of Burgundy

1435 Flanders becomes part of Burgundy. Cultural golden age

1500 Birth of Charles V in Ghent. Brussels becomes the capital

1585 Division of the Netherlands, with the southern part under Spanish rule

per cent of surface area) is sacrificed to their dream every year doesn't seem to preoccupy them unduly. Slightly depressing apartment blocks rise along the coast, and the last dunes between the resorts are hard to make out from afar. New developments and campsites continue to eat into the marsh landscape beyond the dunes, and cars pollute the air.

The economic boom following the war saw increasing urban sprawl in Flanders. On the fringes of historic towns, supermarkets, branches of chain stores, car-repair garages and small factories line broad highways. In a throwback to the industrial barons of the early 20th century, today's factory owners build their ostentatious villas next to the company site. The 'Carpet Boulevard' on the Ghent–Kortrijk motorway is famous. Clever entrepreneurs invented a new weaving technique that conquered the world markets. They were not above showcasing their wealth, which explains the high number of luxury boutiques in Kortrijk and the Ascot aspirations of the *Waregem Koerse* horse race.

A few miles along, the Flemish and visitors alike wrinkle their noses during warm weather in particular: *Het stänkt,* you can smell the intensive farming of poultry, pigs and veal, the production of animal feed, the processing of manure and the slurry in the waterways. Organic agriculture by contrast is not making progress, despite all the publicity drives, and has only managed to grow some 8 per cent over the last decade, to reach 256 farms and 3822 hectares – making up a meagre 0.6 per cent of agriculture. In Wallonia the number is ten times higher.

Despite all the profiteering and laisser-faire, Flanders still has lovely spots too. At Knokke the extensive sandy nature reserve of Zwin shelters numerous breeding birds. Next to that lies a romantic 'polder' landscape of marshy dunes, criss-crossed by

1713 The Spanish Netherlands pass to Austria, and are annexed by France in 1795

1815 United Kingdom of the Netherlands

1830 Revolution - Belgium becomes an independent kingdom

1840 Emergence of the Flemish Movement, beginning of the language dispute

1914–18 German occupation of Belgium. Flemish activists collaborate in the hope of being granted their own state

narrow canals and little cobbled roads. The Westhoek between Ypres and Veurne conveys a feeling of a wide expanse where the Kemmelberg and other hills rising majestically out of the plain, their slopes supporting grapes that produce fine wines. Still, this is a region that can't fail to make you stop and think: countless war cemeteries, from the largest British war cemetery in the world, Tyne Cot, to the German equivalent at Vladslo, remind visitors of the millions who died in First World War. The Verdronken Land van Saeftinghe, an area of mudflats in the shadow of refineries, chemical factories and nuclear power plants in the harbour of Antwerp, reveals the austere poetry of the *plat pays,* immortalised by a famous Jacques Brel chanson. South of Ghent, lovely meadows and deciduous forests surround the artists' colony of Sint-Martens-Latem. The eastern Haspengau region features a sheer endless string of flowering orchards, while in the centre of the Limburg region, the Hoge Kempen national park has been created in rough romantic heathland.

Adorable little spots from the coast to the Haspengau

Not only Flanders' cities and landscapes provide contrasts – so do its customs and lifestyles. Right at the heart of modern business life, old traditions remain alive. In Bruges, the Holy Blood procession provides moments of intense piety, secular festivals such as the *Gentse Feesten* in Ghent or the carnival in Limburg bring whole communities onto the streets. In the villages, old and young breeding courier pigeons. On Saturdays they are trucked far into France and have to race each other home on the Sunday. Another popular leisure activity is cycling, and the performance of the *flandriens,* the Flemish racers, is discussed at length in bars, accompanied by rivers of strong beer from the local breweries.

Alongside this, Flanders has exciting avant-garde culture. Every year, new bands emerge onto the pop and rock scene, and some make their way to international fame. Festivals such as *Rock Werchter* combine young home-grown talent and international stars. At the weekend, Antwerp's buzzing nightlife draws many young Dutch people, while the mega-discos around Kortrijk pull in young French clubbers from the neighbouring Greater Lille area. Since the *Antwerp Six* created a stir at the London fashion

1940–44	1962	1970	1995	2010
German occupation of Belgium, collaboration by Flemish nationalists	Definition of the language demarcation line	Beginning of the conversion of the Belgian centralised state into a federal state	First direct elections to the Vlaamse Raad (regional government)	The Belgian parliamentary elections see the separatist N-VA emerge as the strongest party in Flanders (28 per cent), blocking the formation of a functioning government for 400 days

Kortrijk is a destination for lovers of modern design

fair in 1986, their creations have been a constant presence on the Antwerp catwalk and at shows in Milan, New York and Paris. Hordes of Japanese tourists storm the fashion museum and associ-

Ancient culture and young avant-garde

ated institute and the boutiques of Ann Demeulemeester or Dries Van Noten. Martin Margiela, who was already recycling old clothing and fabrics 20 years ago, now appears downright visionary. And now Bruno Pieters' strict fairtrade and organic designs have raised the bar. Kortrijk too, with its *Biennale Interieur* has blossomed into a destination for lovers of modern design furniture and objects. Arne Quinze is its internationally known figurehead.

Expressive dance and experimental theatre are also thriving on the stage provided by a historic urban landscape. Contemporary visual art is another booming export. Following the example of the patricians of old, Flanders' nouveaux riches are avid collectors, and have long moved beyond home-grown talent such as Panamarenko or Luc Tuymans. Strange as it may sound: the local perspective is a blessing for artistic and cultural progress here. Any town worth its salt builds its own theatres, art museum, cultural or music centre – to the benefit not least of the visitors. While the happening scene might be in the major cities of Antwerp and Ghent, in small towns you will discover treasures and talent. Explore the historic culture by all means, but whatever you do, don't miss the avant-garde!

WHAT'S HOT

1 Roll with it

Active hip Belgians don't use rollerblades, oh no, but roll-erskates *(www.belgiumrollers.com)*, to turn Hasselt, Antwerp, Brussels and the resort of Koksijde into rolling cities. The *Vlaamse Rollerbond (Leuvenselaan 467/14, Tienen, www.rollerbond.be)* is at the heart of the action. This association organises races, acrobatics tournaments and also leisurely trips for rollerskaters, roll-erbladers and skateboarders.

Chocoholics

2

Culinary treats Belgium is famous for its chocolate, and no longer only for its classics, but also for highly unusual blends. Pierre Marcolini *(Avenue Louise 75M, Brussels, photo)*, for instance, mixes pink pepper into the choc mix, while Frederic Blondeel *(Quai aux Briques 24, Brussels)* uses a lot of basil and chilli. The creations of Dominique Persoone *(The Chocolate Line, Simon Stevinplein 19, Bruges)* have been enjoyed by none other than the Rolling Stones. How about wasabi in a chocolate coating?

Brought back to life

3

Art In Belgium, comic characters exist not only between book covers. In Brussels they adorn metro stations – the Stockel station is decorated with images of *Tintin* – or walls; even hot-air balloons in Temse *(www.flyingcomics.be)*. Those who want to discover more comics in the capital can follow the *Comic-Strip-Walk (route: visitbrussels.be, photo)*, starting at the Place de la Bourse. In Antwerp, fans of graphic novels shop at the *Mekanik Comic Shop (Sint-Jacobsmarkt 73, www.ximeralabs.com/mekanik)*.

There are a lot of things to discover in Flanders. A few of the most interesting are listed below

Creative core

Dansaert quarter This neighbourhood in the heart of Brussels is blossoming into a trendy hotspot. Many creative people now live in the area between Boulevard Anspach and the canal, so that even the road surface of Dansaertstrasse now sports an arty pattern. The street is lined with hip shops, such as Idiz Bogam's Vintage boutique *(no. 76)* and *Rue Blanche (no. 39–41)* with its feminine fashion. Once the right outfit has been found, head for *Madame Moustache (Quai au bois à brûler 5–7, photo).* In the dimly lit bar with its lounge and dance floor, DJs make the night pass more quickly than you would like. The crowd is young and trendy.

4

Vintage dreams

We meet again Those who love Antwerp's large flea market will just adore the *Vrijdagmarkt Appartements (bookings through www.i-escape.com).* The flats are in an old townhouse with views of the market and furnished with curious finds from decades past. Maybe the furnishings of the *Hotel Welcome (Quai au bois à brûler 23, Brussels, www.hotelwelcome.com)* were also picked up from the fancy flea market? In any case each of the 17 rooms has its own character. In Ghent you can sleep in a veritable museum. The Art Deco building of the *L'Ecume des Jours (Krijgslaan 4, www.lecumedesjours.com)* is an eyecatcher, as is its interior with matching interior design and an arts exhibition. The exciting dinner to go with all this is served at *Volta (Nieuwe Wandeling 2B),* housed in a former power station.

5

IN A NUTSHELL

BEGUINES

It was around the year 1170 that Maria of Oignies founded the first beguine community, in Liège. As opposed to nuns, these mystics from the upper crust of society would only pledge obedience and chastity. The beguines were free to dispose of their wealth and elected their leader, called the 'Great Lady', who was answerable to the community and could be de-selected. They also chose priests for spiritual support as they saw fit. These emancipated women, engaged in charitable projects, had their own judiciary and were also able to leave the community again. While the movement died out in the 20th century, their tranquil beguine estates, settlements or small towns-within-towns, mostly dating back to the 18th century, remained. They are now part of UNESCO World Heritage.

B.V.

Bekende Vlamingen, 'well-known Flemish people', is the meaning of this common abbreviation. 'Well-known' means those who regularly appear in one of the many Flemish soaps and shows and on *praatprogramma's* (chat shows) on TV in particular. First of all these people are the presenters of the shows, followed by pop singers, politicians, actors, surgeons, thriller writers and university professors, in short anybody who holds some kind of important position in society and is able to chat about sex, money and success.

Photo: Beguine buildings in Aarschot

Oysters, beguines and language disputes: in Flanders, old traditions and modern trends go hand in hand

Unknown Flemish people, by the way, may do that too, to their heart's content, on the radio. No distinction is made here between public (VRT) and commercial broadcasters (VTM). *Ik kwek, dus ik ben* – I hold forth, therefore I am, as a critical columnist once commented. The Flemish after all boast the world's highest level of consumption of this kind of programme, with 70 per cent of the population watching or listening in daily, on average for two-and-a-half hours!

CARS

Before the Second World War, one of the world's most chic and expensive cars, made in Antwerp, was mentioned in the same breath as Rolls-Royce: the Minerva. While the brand didn't survive, the motorcar industry did. Ford, General Motors, Renault and Volvo built large factories in Flanders. Now the Flemings are reconnecting with tradition. Dirk van Braeckel worked his way up at Audi, went on to give Škoda a new image and is now styling the

A controversial hobby: competing for the most beautiful finch song

exciting new Bentley luxury models. Having also started at Audi and Škoda, Luc Donckerwolke went on to be design director at Lamborghini and Seat. Since 2011 he has been director of advanced design at VW. Steven Crijns styles the bodywork at Lotus. After being at the helm of Pininfarina between 2007 to 2011, Lowie Vermeersch now designs car bodies in his own Granstudio.

DANCE & THEATRE

Flemish choreographers and directors are sought-after and jet around the globe. Jan Fabre, who is also very successful as a visual artist, is the undisputed star amongst stars. The top choreographers include Alain Platel and Wim Vandekeybus – as well as Anne Teresa De Keersmaeker, who also trains the new generation in her dancing school *P.A.R.T.S.* One of the biggest new talents is Sidi Larbi Cherkaoui. Guy Cassiers, director of *Het Toneelhuis* in Antwerp, and Jan Lauwers with his *Needcompany* are darlings of the international theatre festivals. Top opera houses around the globe compete to get Guy Joosten and Ivo van Hove to stage works for them. Tom Lanoye ('Fortress Europe', 'Mephisto Forever', 'Battles!') is a feted author.

FEDERALISM

The Kingdom of Belgium that emerged in 1830 was a centralised state in the same way as France, consisting of nine administrative provinces, comparable to the French *départements*. Since 1970 the kingdom has been converted into a federal state, step by step. There are four regions (roughly comparable to Swiss cantons) with their directly elected parliaments and regional governments: Brussels, the small German-speaking area, Flanders and Wallonia. Flanders has five provinces: Antwerp, Flemish Brabant (capital: Leuven), Limburg (Hasselt),

East Flanders (Ghent) and West Flanders (Bruges).

FIGHTING FINCHES

A little furtively, an estimated 20,000 Flemish people cultivate a leisure activity which was documented as far back as 1595 in Ypres and has entered several popular sayings. In the spring, they lock male finches into small wooden cages with only two openings to let in some light and air, and drive them to the edge of a quiet street or field. The birds soon start singing their little hearts out. The sound their captors listen out for *suskewiet*, which is considered a truly Flemish song (Wallonian finches say *djut*), and is ideally trilled twenty times a minute. The champions later take part in a big competition. This sport of ordinary Flemish people is controversial however. Many *vinkeniers (www.avibo.be)* refuse to breed the finches, because that would mean their champions couldn't take part in the competitions. So finches are imported from Russia – or caught illegally in Belgium, attracting protests from bird conservationists.

FLEMISH FOODIES

In 2003, the gourmets first discovered a young chef in Dranouter, near the French border, who was transforming regional seasonal produce into exciting creations: Kobe Desramaults. He picked up tips and tricks and his state-of-the-art technique from Sergio Herman at *Oud Sluis* and a hip restaurant in Barcelona. Like an archaeologist Desramaults hunts down old recipes and rare vegetables, cereals and fruit, meat, cheeses and wild herbs in the Heuvelland. His findings and ideas are given an enthusiastic reception from farmers – and a few other brilliant young chefs. First calling themselves *The Flemish Primitives*, they now go by the name of *Flemish Foodies*. First they created in stir in Bruges, then in Ghent. Today, the *Local Food Express* network of small organic producers built up by Kobe Desramaults in the Heuvelland delivers fresh produce with the true taste of real food to a dozen restaurants.

JAINS

Quiet industry They came inconspicuously from the early 1970s onwards: diamond traders from the western Indian federal state of Gujarat. They are Jains. Non-violence is at the centre of their religion, which means that they are not only vegetarians but may not even eat root vegetables nor onions, as little animals could be hidden inside. Today about 300 Jain families control three quarters of Antwerp's diamond trade. The Jains themselves attribute their success to good karma. Experts say it is their idea of having even the smallest stones polished and made into jewellery back home at rock-bottom prices, round-the-clock online trading, and their global networks. The closed community lives in the fine residential district of Wilrijk; their lives revolve around a spectacular temple and arts centre built from snow-white marble, as well as the cricket pitch next to it *(Laarstraat 20 | short.travel/fla1)*.

LANGUAGE DISPUTES

French was the official language in the Kingdom of Belgium – and that included Flanders. Flemish teachers and chaplains were not happy. Founding the Flemish Movement in 1840, they demanded the recognition and promotion of their mother tongue. After all, even then, more Flemish-speakers than Francophones lived in the kingdom. The stronger democracy became – in 1918 all adult men were given the vote, in 1948 the women too – the more the Flemish language took over in all areas of public life in Flanders. In 1962, the long-established linguistic frontier between Flanders and the Francophone part of Belgium was enshrined in law. Brussels and six residential suburbs which were predominantly French-speaking, became officially bilingual. In a few villages and small towns on the language border (such as Ronse in east Flanders for instance, or Enghien in Hainaut) the minority may use their mother tongue when dealing with the authorities or in school. Visitors will note that in day-to-day life the Belgians are flexible. In the Ardennes the Flemish are served in their own language just as easily as the Walloons are in French when they visit the coast.

NOUVEAUX RICHES

In the 19th century, Flanders was a poor rural region. Many Flemings were migrant workers in Wallonian coal pits or seasonal agricultural hands in the north of France. The Flemish maids and cleaning women, bakers and butchers became legendary in Brussels. This all changed in the 1960s. While all the pits were shut down in Wallonia, and many steel works closed, the Flemish ports of Antwerp, Ghent and Zeebrugge saw heavy expansion. Major firms such as BASF and General Motors started producing there. Hardworking Flemish people founded small companies. The region blossomed – to such an extent that workers had to be hired from Morocco and Turkey. The Flemish population was soon proudly displaying its new-found wealth with houses, cars and yachts, golf courses and top restaurants.

OYSTERS & MUSSELS

Seafood forms part of Flemish day-to-day fare. Most is imported, though some local produce too comes onto the market. In the Spuikom behind the harbour of Oostende – a wide basin between port, canals and polder dune marshes with its own particular blend of sea and fresh water - the fabulous oysters that were appreciated as early as 1900 under the name of ostendaises are thriving once again. A special kind of algae gives them a green colour. Off Nieuwpoort and Knokke, structures with long steel cables support mussels of the finest quality, fleshy and nicely salty. Here too production is rising year on year. This success is in great part due to the experts of the Vlaams Instituut voor de Zeevisserij in Oostende, who are already thinking up new cultivation projects.

POLYPHONY

Between the 14th and the 16th century, Franco-Flemish polyphonists had a dominant position in European music. Trained at the cathedrals of Antwerp, Bruges and Cambrai, Josquin Desprez, Adriaan Willaert and Orlando di Lasso prospered at royal courts from London to Naples with their new, virtuoso polyphonic compositions. Amongst the highlights are Orlando di Lasso's 'Tears of Saint Peter' and his setting of Petrarch's poems. Since 1964 the *Festival Musica Antiqua* in Bruges has been staging this music for a wider audience, and thanks to an international competition, brings forth new young artists from all over the globe. The scene's undisputed star is Paul van

Nevel with his *Huelgas Ensemble of crystal-clear voices.* Again and again this Flemish maestro has discovered new scores in archives, often by unjustly forgotten polyphonists.

TAALUNIE

Since 1980 Flanders and the Netherlands have formed a 'Dutch Language Union', agreeing in a bilateral contract to address together all questions pertaining to their shared High Dutch language. In 2003 the Republic of Surinam joined the Taalunie. Renowned linguists give recognition to new expressions and work out rules, which are made into law by parliament and supervised by a general secretariat (headquartered in Den Haag). Still it is notable that Flanders and the Netherlands are drifting apart linguistically under the influence of modern media. In Flanders you'll hear more dialect being spoken, whilst in the Netherlands a somewhat Americanised Dutch is gaining ground. Flemish films and TV series are now subtitled before being broadcast in the Netherlands.

VLAAMS BELANG

In 1978 extreme-right Flemings founded the *Vlaams Blok party.* Slogans such as 'Flemish Flanders!' or 'Foreigners out!' brought them more votes with every election. In 2004, open racism led to condemnation by the Supreme Court, a change of name (Vlaams Belang) and the best election result ever: 24 per cent at the regional elections. In 2006, the racially motivated murder of a sympathiser spelt the beginning of a downturn. First the voters, then high-ranking party members too, changed over to the *Nieuw-Vlaamse Alliantie (N-VA).* In Belgian parliamentary elections, the N-VA became the strongest political force in Flanders (28 per cent). The local elections 2012 confirmed this trend, and the N-VA now provides the mayor in Antwerp (38 per cent), for instance. The most important goal on the N-VA's agenda is to break up Belgium and found an independent Republic of Flanders. In other policies, the N-VA is characterised by social conservatism.

URBAN GARDENING

When the EU regional commission moved into a freshly renovated building on Brussels' Rue Belliard in 2004, the façade designed by architects Art & Build created a real stir: behind glass walls, bamboo shrubs that improve air quality inside were grew rampant – an original method of vertical greening. This example has since found many followers. In Brussels, Ghent and Antwerp, flat roofs, terraces and small balconies are transformed into meadows and vegetable gardens, with bee hives placed in between. Community allotments are emerging at park corners, on derelict plots, and in empty factory halls, partly with the active support of the communal administration. Weeding, seeding and harvesting – and occasionally cooking and eating together afterwards– make a healthy contribution to the social fabric of anonymous big cities.

FOOD & DRINK

They are well-known from museums: lush paintings by Flemish masters telling of epic sessions of wining and dining? Jan Fyt and Frans Snijders were the masters of still-lifes featuring dead game, while Pieter Aertsen and Joachim Beuckelaer created the new genre of kitchen and larder scenes.

The Brueghel and Teniers dynasties immortalised countless banquets. Much later, James Ensor's 'Oyster Eater' created controversy for portraying the uninhibited enjoyment of those aphrodisiac molluscs.

Today, the Flemish passion for good food and drink is no longer painted but documented on television. Every broadcaster has its own cook or pastry chef, with Wim Ballieu, Piet Huysentruyt, Wim Meeus and Peter van Asbroeck amongst the *Bekende Vlamingen*. Their cookbooks sell like the proverbial hot cakes. Programmes with a competitive slant, such as 'De beste hobbykok van Vlaanderen', 'Mijn restaurant' or 'Komen eten' achieve top ratings. Michelin-starred chef Peter Goossens even founded his own cookery channel, *Njam*. Every daily newspaper and every magazine has a restaurant section.

On weekdays the Flemish cook and eat quickly. Students and the workers lunch in the canteen or a snack bar, but at weekends they make up for lost time. Restaurants are fully booked, and a Saturday night amongst friends and Sunday dinner with the family have a long tradition. That is when some Flemish

Photo: 'Mechelse Koekoek'

Of gourmets and gourmands: Flanders' cuisine offers plenty of delicacies – from rustic to elegant

people also take a hearty breakfast, with fried black pudding and veal sausage, bacon, scrambled eggs and cheese, or start the day elegantly with croissants and *pateekes* (tartlets). Another favourite is *krentenbrood,* a fluffy currant loaf served with fresh country butter. Part of the weekend ritual is to visit a pub-restaurant – called *café* – for strong beer and a chat.

At family parties and public holidays, the Flemish party hard and prove themselves to be true *lekkerbekken,* gourmets. If you want to go out for a meal you'll be spoilt for choice, from a simple *eetcafé* to a refined Michelin-starred restaurant run by a creative head chef. No wonder that there are many gourmet establishments even in smaller towns and in the country side celebrating the art of haute cuisine using local produce. Here in particular the Flemish are prepared to pay good money for good food. Here's our tip: most starred restaurants serve a lunch that is much cheaper than the evening menu. And

LOCAL SPECIALITIES

▶ **Asperges à la flamande** – asparagus in melted butter with boiled chopped-up eggs and parsley
▶ **Cabillaud à la bière** – codfish, cooked in beer with bits of bacon
▶ **Carbonnades flamandes** – beef or pork goulash, braised with vegetables, in beer (also called stoofvlees; photo right)
▶ **Faisan à la brabançonne** – roast pheasant with braised chicory
▶ **Garnaalkroketten** – cream croquettes with North Sea prawns
▶ **Hutsepot** – stew with various types of meat and vegetables
▶ **Konijn op z'n Vlaams** – rabbit braised in beer, sometimes served with prunes or sour cherries
▶ **Mechelse Koekoek** – select chicken braised in beer with smoked bacon or in a cream sauce with mushrooms
▶ **Mosselen met frietjes** – mussels cooked in a vegetable broth (sometimes with white wine) (photo left), served with fries

▶ **Paling in 't groen** – eel in thick parsley sauce
▶ **Pens** – black pudding or veal sausage, often grilled, with stewed apples and mashed potato
▶ **Rijstpap** – sweet rice with vanilla, sometimes made with saffron or raisins
▶ **Rog met kapertjes** – skate wings, fried in butter and served with capers
▶ **Schelvis in mosterdsaus** – steamed haddock in mustard sauce
▶ **Sole meunière** – sole fried in butter
▶ **Sole ostendaise** – steamed sole in a cream sauce with seafood
▶ **Tomates crevettes** – raw tomatoes filled with prawns
▶ **Vleesballetjes met krieken** – small meatballs in sour cherry sauce
▶ **Waterzooi** – fish or chicken, in a soup with vegetables and cream
▶ **Witloof** – chicory, braised, fried or oven-roasted with ham and cheese on top

set meals are always better value than three courses à la carte.
A quick look at any local menu reveals that fish and meat weigh in about equally. Local fishermen take their daily catch to specialised markets in Oostende, Nieuwpoort and Zeebrugge. Sole and prawns come from Flemish waters, cod, haddock and herring from the North Sea. Lobster, mussels and oysters

are imported from France and Zeeland. An expensive delicacy now much appreciated abroad is *royal Belgian caviar* cultivated at a sturgeon farm in Turnhout. Foreign palates particularly enjoy trying fish or mussels prepared with beer or served with cheese.

The most popular types of meat are beef (the finest breed being the local *blanc-bleu belge)*, pork, horse, rabbit and chicken, as well as local game: duck, hare and pheasant, also often braised in beer. The usual accompaniment is potatoes, from floury boiled potatoes and creamy mash to crispy croquettes and golden pommes frites.

Despite all the trends in the shape of *Veggiedag, Flemish Foodies* or *Urban Gardening,* all exhortations on television and in cookbooks: little fruit and veg finds its way onto the table of Flemish people, even though the region produces tons of it. Exceptions such as asparagus and chicory or the divine Léopold grapes from the greenhouses of Hoeilaart only confirm the rule: *Da 's voor de gâât,* 'fruit and vegetables are for goats'. The seasonal organic produce regularly promoted by publicity campaigns is only bought by a small urban elite.

The wines that Flemish people traditionally prefer to accompany their food come from the Bordeaux regions. Yet the – substantial – consumption of wine remains far below that of the local beers. While not every village has its own brewery any longer, the choice and variety are far superior to what other countries produce. Pilsner, *kriek* (fermented with cherry juice) and *witbier* (spiced, cloudy wheat beer) will slake sudden attacks of thirst. Strong light beers such as *Duvel* or *Delirium tremens* lend wings to the conversation, while the dark, aromatic, high-octane abbey

beers are appreciated by fine palates. The best brands are brewed by the strict Trappist fathers themselves in monasteries (in Achel, Westmalle and Westvleteren). Gourmets swear by the combination of heavy beer and soft cheese. *Brugs beschuit,* a slightly spicy, sweet

Laid-back and cosy: coffee break in Ghent

twice-baked toast, completes the feast. In some parts of Flanders two more specialities have maintained themselves: genever, a grain-based spirit flavoured with juniper berries, is popular in Limburg and east Flanders in particular; well-cooled *borreltje* is served both as an aperitif and as a digestif. Elderly ladies of the bourgeoisie take the occasional sip of a glass of *Elixir d'Anvers* or *Elixir Oud Gent* (herbal liqueur).

SHOPPING

Shops are usually open Mon–Sat 10am–6pm, shopping centres 9am–7pm or 8pm. In the big cities, many bakers, butchers and corner shops are open on Sundays too, as are a number of boutiques in the resorts. You'll find plenty of night shops. In small towns and villages, nearly all shops are closed for lunch.

ANTIQUES

Flanders has the finest antique shops you could wish for, in Antwerp and Bruges in particular. For cheaper bric-a-brac head for the Sunday market in Tongeren, the weekend markets in Antwerp and Ghent, as well as the *Rommelmarkten* (taking place in all towns and cities, in spring/autumn in particular).

ART & DESIGN

The gallery density is pretty high in Antwerp and Ghent, with prices to match. You'll spend much less purchasing graphic work, even by well-known artists, in the INSIDER TIP shops of the museums dedicated to modern art (MuHKA Antwerp, Mu.Zee Oostende, S.M.A.K. Ghent). Flemish design is a well-kept secret. If funds don't stretch to an expensive couch

by Arne Quinze, this star designer also produces nice side tables and stools. Creative young Flemings are designing great affordable objects such as candlesticks, fruit bowls or vases in limited numbers. A top name here is Bram Boo. Last not least: bed linen or tablecloths made from the finest linen by the traditional western Flemish manufacturers *De Witte Lietaer* or *Libeco*.

CULINARY TREATS

The hand-crafted strong beers (and the glasses that go with them) by microbreweries or the Trappist monasteries of Achel, Westmalle and Westvleteren, as well as unusual chocolates by creative confiseurs, make popular souvenirs. The delicately spiced *speculoos* biscuits and the strong *peperkoek* (a kind of gingerbread) also count amongst the classics. Beauvoorde and Ypres are famous for meat pastries and cheese. Aromatic raw-milk cheeses are left to mature slowly in Ghent *(Het Hinkelspel)* and Limburg *(Kaasmakerij Catharinadal)*. For generations small producers in Ghent and Tongeren have been making hot mustard, used to preserve vegetables *(pickles)* or fruit *(mosterdfruit)*. The Haspengouw produces fresh fruit

Delicatessen and design: whether sweet treats, top fashion or electro sounds – the range of Flemish specialities is guaranteed to entice you

juices, exquisite Chardonnay, delicious jams, and aromatic apple and pear brandy. The most expensive fruit ripen in hothouses in Hoeilaart and Overijse south of Brussels: thick, sweet table grapes, packed in fancy silk paper. In *Ghent* and Hasselt they distil *genever*, often perfumed with juniper berries, apple or lemon. Another citrus-scented product is the *Elixir d'Anvers liqueur*. An exclusive choice is INSIDERTIP *Royal Belgian Caviar* from Turnhout, an unusual one the sparkling wine *Chardonnay Meerdael* made using the champagne method (Oud-Heverlee near Leuven), *Wiscoutre Brut* (Heuvelland) or *Rosé Parel Brut* (Genoels-Elderen, Limburg).

FASHION

Antwerp's fashion designers have turned their city into a mecca for *fashion*. Ann Demeulemeester, Dries Van Noten, but also up-and-coming talents run chic boutiques. ☺ INSIDERTIP Bruno Pieters' 'Honest by' line has created the new trend

in fashion, committed to fair trade and organic agriculture. Backpacks by Hedgren, Kipling and Eastpak are extremely popular. The most demanding fashionistas will find what they're looking for in Knokke-Het Zoute, and Hasselt too has a certain scene, though more modest.

MUSIC

Music lovers will find strong Flemish presence in pop and rock. Arno likes to sing about the Oostende of days gone by, Flip Koweliers and the *Fixkes* murmur love songs or protest songs in West Flemish. Ozark Henry is top in soft pop. Helmut Lotti moves the older generation, and *Clouseau* or *dEUS* are the favourites of the middle-aged generation. Young people enjoy Puerto Rican-born Gabriel Ríos, *Gotye*, *Milow* and *Netsky*. The electro sounds by *Hooverphonic* can stand up to international comparison. The best record stores can be found in Antwerp, Bruges, Ghent and Hasselt.

THE PERFECT ROUTE

BACK TO THE ROOTS

① *Tongeren* → p. 89 makes the ideal starting point: Flanders oldest town was founded in 55 BC by the Romans. The *Gallo-Romeins Museum* is a lively introduction to the local history. Next door, the *Onze-Lieve-Vrouwebasiliek* was the region's first bishop's seat in the 4th century. On your way to the station you should stop at *Blanckaert's* to try a *Limburgs Vlaaike* (fruit cake). After that, the intercity train crosses fields, meadows, forests and even some vineyards to take you to **②** *Leuven* → p. 64. The students at the university, which dates back to 1425, bring life to this small town. The Gothic *Stadhuis* and *Sint-Pieterskerk* are a reminder of the town's proud history as the cradle of the Duchy of Brabant. From Leuven take the train via Bruxelles Aéroport National and Mechelen to Antwerp.

BAROQUE, DIAMONDS AND FASHION

In **③** *Antwerp* → p. 68 visitors are greeted by the imposing *Centraal Station* and the bustling *Diamantwijk* in its shadow. The strolling and shopping streets De Keyserlei and Meir will lead you to the *Onze-Lieve-Vrouwekathedraal* and *Grote Markt* (photo above). The *MAS (Museum aan de Stroom)* commands panoramic views of the city and port and their surroundings, as well as the hip *'t Eilandje* neighbourhood. For a contrasting experience, why not visit the Baroque-era *Rubenshuis* and a leisurely shopping spree through the fashion district around Nationalestraat. A few steps from Ann Demeulemeester's boutique, relax in the hip winebar *The Glorious*.

CULTURAL AND CULINARY

Factories and large-scale nurseries line the train route from Antwerp to **④** *Ghent* → p. 48. Take tram no. 1 to the Art Deco station for the *S.M.A.K.* and its collection of contemporary art. The vibrant university quarter takes you to the *Sint-Baafskathedraal* with its world-famous Ghent Altarpiece. On your way you might like to pick up some original chocolates from *Yuzu's* and then, after the walk past the *belfry* and the *Sint-Niklaaskerk,* hot mustard from *Vve. Tierentyn-Verlent*. On the way to *Gravensteen* consider a detour to the *design museum*. After that, you've earned a cocktail prepared with Ghent genever at *Jigger's*, before tasting Flemish avant-garde cuisine at *j.e.f.'s*.

Experience the many faces of Flanders, its old churches and wide coast, on a rail journey zig-zagging from east to west

TO THE NORTH SEA COAST

On the journey aboard the train to De Panne, the lovely Leie valley and later the barer polder landscape glides past. The quiet town of ⑤ *Veurne* → p. 47 is worth stopping at to discover the tower and square that once inspired the famous German poet Rainer Maria Rilke. At De Panne train station change onto the Kusttram. Past apartment blocks, dunes and beaches, Nieuwpoort's marina and what remains of the Atlantikwall, German defences from the last war, you reach ⑥ *Oostende* → p. 44. The restaurant *Ostend Queen* offers panoramic views to accompany its fish dishes. A visit to the *James Ensorhuis* conjures up memories of the Belle Époque, which in fact is still completely intact at ⑦ *De Haan* → p. 41 (photo below left). At Blankenberge train station then board the intercity train to Bruges.

THE PRETTIEST TOWN IN FLANDERS

In ⑧ *Bruges* → p. 32 take a stroll through the greenery via Begijnvest to the romantic *Minnewater* and from there on to the picturesque *Begijnhof.* Follow the stream of visitors to the *Onze-Lieve-Vrouwekerk,* where you should take a little time to appreciate Michelangelo's Madonna before continuing to the *market* and *belfry.* On the way to the *Sint-Sebastiaansgilde* you'll have time to see patrician palaces and squares, canals and working families' homes, as well as fortifying yourself with Bruges specialities in the *Refter* restaurant. Before returning make sure to buy speculoos biscuits and gingerbread from *Juliette's!*

400 km/250 miles. Duration six hours. Detailed map of the route on the back cover, in the road atlas and the pull-out map.

BRUGES AND WEST FLANDERS

West Flanders is a province shaped by tourism through and through. Medieval Bruges attracts millions of visitors from all over the world.

Smaller towns such as Veurne are also very popular, followed by the 64km/40-mile coastal strip, with the *Oostkust* on the one side of Oostende, and the *Westkust* on the other. The coast might be chronically built up, but the Belgians love it: the diffuse light and strong breeze on the English Channel, the happy buzz at the beach and on the promenades. A modern light railway, the Kusttram, its 70 stops close to the beaches and town centres, runs along the entire coastline. Extending between the coast and cities of art, vast polder marsh landscapes feature romantic canals, neat villages and

stately churches. In the southwest the polder landscape gradually gives way to the hilly country around the Kemmelberg. This is where the hops are grown that go into the strong beers, and where blue-flowering flax serves as a reminder that West Flanders owed its immense wealth to fabrics and the drapery trade.

BRUGES

MAP INSIDE BACK COVER
(125 D2) *(∅ D4)* **Beautiful Bruges is what the locals – 'Bruggelingen', of whom 35,000 live in the historical centre – call their town.**

No other town in Flanders has as many well-preserved old buildings as Bruges.

Culture and nature: West Flanders is a landscape of red walls, white beaches and the green polder marshes

CITY WHERE TO START?
Market square: All streets lead to the market with the belfry. Stadhuis, Onze-Lieve-Vrouwekerk and Begijnhof, as well as the shopping district can be reached on foot from here. Park your car in one of the multi-storey car-parks at the railway station or below the Zand, from where buses nos. 0, 1, 3, 4, 6, 11, 12 and 13 go to the market square.

The façades are reflected in the canals, and towers rise majestically out of the urban landscape. The city owes its splendour to its medieval port. In the Middle Ages, Bruges was the hub connecting the northern European cities of the Hanseatic League and the trading cities of southern Europe. Merchants and bankers employed the greatest artists of their time: Hans Memling, Jan van Eyck, Michelangelo. When access to the North Sea silted up, the city fell into long sleep, and had to wait for the 19th century and

The Begijnhof ten Wijngaarde is a small tranquil town within a town

the founding of the new port of Zeebrugge to rise again. Now, the old and the new form a harmonious backdrop. Behind the façades, countless artworks await the visitor – and in the evening, there are cultural events and entertainment.

SIGHTSEEING

BEGIJNHOF TEN WIJNGAARDE ★
Grouped around an extensive lawn sprinkled with blooming daffodils, the whitewashed houses seem timeless. Today Benedictine sisters live and pray here. *Daily 6.30am–6.30pm | Wijngaardstraat*

BELFORT EN HALLEN ★ ⚄
In the 13th century, the good citizens of Bruges erected their mighty belfry, dominating the extensive market square, and

the cloth hall. The treasury on the second floor guards the documents granting Bruges town status. There are fabulous views from the viewing platform by the glockenspiel, and regular concerts too. *Belfry daily 9.30am–5pm, concerts 15 June–Sept Mon, Wed, Sat 9pm, Oct–14 June Wed, Sat 2.15pm | admission 8 euros | Markt*

INSIDER TIP FRIETMUSEUM
The exhibition in a splendid 14th-century merchant's office documents the origins of the potato in Peru, its distribution and cultivation, the Belgian invention of fries and their conquest of the world – in the arts and comics, too. Samples are available in the cellar. *Closed 24–26 Dec and 31 Dec–15 Jan, otherwise daily 10am–5pm | admission 6 euros | Vlamingstraat 33 | www.frietmuseum.be*

GROENINGEMUSEUM ⭐

The white rooms of this art museum truly bring out the power of masterpieces of old Dutch painting. Amongst the highlights are 'The Virgin and Child with Joris van der Paele' by Jan van Eyck and the 'Last Judgement' by Hieronymus Bosch. Also on display: works produced between the 17th and 20th centuries, as well as by the Bruges-born Art Nouveau artist Frank Brangwyn. Tue–Sun 9.30am–5pm | admission 8 euros | Dijver 12

HEILIG BLOEDBASILIEK

The ground floor is the oldest church in Bruges (construction was started in 1139). Resting on massive pillars, the vault and side chapels were built in strict Romanesque style. Later, a further room was added above, housing a relic said to contain a drop of the blood of Christ. Daily, 9.30–12 noon and 2–5pm | free admission | Burg

MEMLINGMUSEUM

The museum in the chapel of the Romanesque Sint-Janshospitaal is an introduction to the life and artistic scene of medieval Bruges. The highlight are six works by Hans Memling, amongst them the 'St Ursula Shrine' with its miniatures. Also worth seeing: the pharmacy and the offices. Tue–Sun 9.30am–5pm | admission 8 euros | Mariastraat 38

INSIDER TIP ▶ MUSEUM SINT-SEBASTIAANSGILDE

In the building of the ancient archers' guild, documents and precious gifts serve to illustrate Bruges' eminent position. The king of Belgium and Queen Elizabeth II are members of the guild. The large romantic ● gardens offer views of the windmills along the canal and the Renaissance tower of the archers' guildhall. The divine calm is only broken every quarter-hour by the delicate glockenspiel. June–Sept Tue–Thu 10am–12 noon, Sat

---

⭐ Begijnhof Ten Wijngaarde
Prayers are still said in Flanders' most beautiful 'béguinage' as the French say in Bruges → p. 34

⭐ Belfort en Hallen
Sublime testimony to the power of the burghers of Bruges – glockenspiel included → p. 34

⭐ Groeningemuseum
Traditional museum in Bruges showing masterpieces of old Dutch painting to Art Nouveau → p. 35

⭐ Onze-Lieve-Vrouwekerk
Gothic church in Bruges with Burgundian dynastic tombs and a Madonna by Michelangelo → p. 36

⭐ Stadhuis
In Bruges, Belgium's oldest town hall bears witness to historic wealth → p. 36

⭐ Lakenhal
Rebuilt in 1925 to sublime splendour: the Gothic cloth hall in Ypres → p. 43

⭐ Veurne
A bulky church tower, cheerful stepped gables and an elegant belfry → p. 47

⭐ Vladslo
The graves of German soldiers are guarded by the moving 'Mourning Parents' by Käthe Kollwitz → p. 47

MARCO POLO HIGHLIGHTS

2–5pm, Oct–May Tue–Thu, Sat 2–5pm | admission 3 euros | Carmersstraat 174 | www.sebastiaansgilde.be

ONZE-LIEVE-VROUWEKERK ★

In the Gothic Church of Our Lady with its striking spire you can admire the charming 'Virgin with Child' by Michelangelo and the impressive tombs of Charles the Bold, Duke of Burgundy, and his daughter Mary of Burgundy, worked in marble and brass. *Tue–Sat 9.30am–5pm, Sun 1.30–5pm | admission 4 euros | Mariastraat*

STADHUIS ★

Bruges boasts the oldest town hall in Belgium (1376). A monumental staircase leads into its Gothic hall with a richly carved, painted and gilded wooden vaulted ceiling and ancient sculptures. The left-hand wing, the *Brugse Vrije,* is where the territories of the city were administered, and courts of law sat. The jury members met in the opulent Renaissance hall with its huge fireplace and tapestry-clad walls. *Daily 9.30am–5pm | admission 2 euros | Burg*

Graceful image in Bruges' Church of Our Lady: the 'Madonna and Child' by Michelangelo

SINT-SALVATORSKATHEDRAAL

Above the splendid choir stalls of the cathedral dedicated to St Saviour, or the Redeemer, coats of arms serve as a reminder of the 13th session of the exclusive knight's Order of the Golden Fleece. Note also the tapestries from Brussels showing scenes from the life of Christ, as well as the Renaissance retable, or altar screen, reliquary shrines and tombs in the side choir chapels. *Sun–Fri 2–5pm | admission 2.50 euros | Sint-Salvatorskerkhof*

FOOD & DRINK

INSIDER TIP **DE HALVE MAAN**

The fine if fairly strong *Brugse Zot* and *Straffe Hendrik* beers are brewed in a 19th-century building. To mop up the alcohol, they serve tasty home-made fare both inside the tavern and in the beer garden. *Daily | Walplein 26 | tel. 050 44 42 22 | www.halvemaan.be | Budget*

HERTOG JAN

Gert De Mengeleer is a leading representative of molecular cuisine. You can watch him work his very precise magic from the tables along the glass kitchen wall. Berries, vegetables and herbs come fresh from his nearby farm. *Closed Sun/ Mon | Torhoutsesteenweg 479 | tel. 050 67 34 45 | www.hertog-jan.com | Expensive*

PÂTISSERIE SERVAIS VAN MULLEM

Elegant café by the theatre. Delicious pastries, discreet classical music, classy service. *Closed Tue | Vlamingstraat 56 | tel. 050 33 05 15*

INSIDER TIP REFTER

Michelin-starred chef Geert van Hecke serves clever brasserie food in this chic satellite operation. Choose the terrace for a fabulous place to dine. *Closed Sun/ Mon | Molenmeers 2 | tel. 050 44 49 00 | www.bistrorefter.com | Moderate*

SHOPPING

The shopping zone occupying the area between *Noordzandstraat*, *Geldmuntstraat*, *Zuidzandstraat* and *Steenstraat*asis is mainly geared towards mass tourism, with a few more exclusive shops near the *market*.

CALLEBERT

Here you'll find a huge selection of (smaller) design objects. There is a big section for children too. Regular exhibitions, café and wine bar on the roof terrace. *Wollestraat 25 | www.callebert.be*

HOET (THEO)

Aspiring to join the Flemish in-crowd? Just purchase a pair of these extravagant (sun) glasses. *Vlamingstraat 19*

INSIDER TIP JULIETTE'S

This small shop sells hand-made, unusually spiced speculoos biscuits and gingerbread, nicely gift-wrapped too. *Wollestraat 31A*

ROMBAUX

Fabulous choice of vinyl and CDs, from classics to pop. *Mallebergplaats 13*

LEISURE & WELL-BEING

BRUGS OMMELAND

The atmospheric surroundings of Bruges – with canals, polder landscape, palaces and little forests – are ideal for bike tours. The *Fietspunt rent-a-bike (Mon–Fri 7.30am–7pm, Sat–Sun 9am–9.40pm)* next to the train station hires out bikes (daily rate 12 euros), and you can pick up a free detailed map from the *Infokantoor* next door.

INSIDER TIP SENSES

This spa and beauty parlour is one of the few offering treatments and massages with chocolate and cocoa butter. *Torhoutsesteenweg 503 | tel. 050 30 05 35 | short. travel/fla2*

ENTERTAINMENT

Bruges actually has a pretty good nightlife as well. At the *Eiermarkt (Egg Market)*, in *Kuipersstraat* and in *Langestraat*, numerous pubs and clubs playing various musical styles attract a young crowd, between Thu and Sat in particular.

CONCERTGEBOUW

In the large and small hall of this impressive concert venue designed by architects Robbrecht & Daem, classical music rules the roost generally. Don't miss Jos van Immerseel and his Anima Aeterna orchestra. *'t Zand 34 | tel. 070 22 33 02 | www.concertgebouw.be*

ENTREPOT

At weekends, this former depot in the port area houses the coolest parties with live music of various persuasions. *Binnenweg 4 | www.hetentrepot.be*

INSIDER TIP **DE REPUBLIEK**

A rendezvous for bohemians with a good range of Belgian beers, exotically inspired dishes (incl. vegetarian), and cocktails. Atmospheric courtyard. *Daily 11am–4am | Sint-Jakobsstraat 36*

DE STOEPA

A friendly hostelry with garden, frequented by young people from Bruges. Good vibes. *Daily 11am–3am | Oostmers 124*

WHERE TO STAY

At weekends, rates for the over 120 hotels and nearly as many bed & breakfast houses usually go up. Often a minimum stay of two nights is stipulated. *www.brugge-bedandbreakfast.com* presents the places on offer in detail. Find a large range of holiday villas in the town at *www.belvilla.de.*

ADORNES ⁓

Three step-gabled houses with gorgeous views of the canals. Modern rooms, the finest under a high-beamed ceiling. Good buffet breakfast, hotel car park and guest bikes. *20 rooms | Sint-Annarei 26 | tel. 050 341336 | www.adornes.be | Moderate*

DE DRIE KONINGEN

The six perfectly appointed apartments with 1–4 bedrooms housed in three medieval houses, restored with excellent taste and boasting a garden, are ideal for longer stays. Hotel garage spaces, a small pool and a nice bar are welcome extras, and the castle and market are only a few paces away. *Twijnstraat 13–17 | tel. 050 675513 | www.dedriekoningen.be | Moderate*

HOTEL DE GOEZEPUT ⁓

This 18th-century house in a quiet side street is only a stone's throw from Onze-Lieve-Vrouwekerk and Sint-Salvatorkathedraal, and its comfortable rooms under old beams offer fine views. Modern lounge with open fire, terrace and a corner where children can play. *15 rooms | Goezeputstraat 29 | tel. 050 342694 | www.hotelgoezeput.be | Budget*

HOTEL MONTANUS

An old patrician house and a colonial-style villa with 1200 sq m gardens in between. Generously sized rooms in various styles. INSIDER TIP Breakfast served till noon, picnic basket and guest bikes. *13 rooms | Nieuwe Gentweg 78 | tel. 050 331176 | www.montanus.be | Expensive*

INFORMATION

Toerisme Brugge – In & Uit | 't Zand 34 | tel. 050 444646 | www.brugge.be/toerisme

WHERE TO GO

DAMME (125 D2) (*Ø E3*)

This little town (pop. 11,000) is a popular day-trip destination 5 km/3 miles northeast of Bruges. Boats plying a pretty canal connect the two towns *(departure Noorweegse Kaai in Bruges | April–Sept daily 10am, 12 noon, 2pm, 4pm, 6pm | return ticket 7 euros)*. Damme, once a trading hub for Bordeaux wine and port wine, has star-shaped town walls, the Gothic *Church of Our Lady*, the *Sint-Janshospitaal* and the late Gothic *town hall*. The birthplace of poet Jacob van Maerlant (1235–1300) maintains its reputation as a town of books (every 2nd Sun of the month, a *book market* takes place on the market square). In the picaresque novel by Charles De Coster, the prankster *Tijl Uilenspiegel* was born in Damme. *Information: Toerisme Damme | Jacob van Maerlantstraat 3 | tel. 050 28 86 10 | www.toerismedamme.be*

KNOKKE-HEIST

(125 D1) (*🔲 D–E 2–3*) The fanciest sea resort on the Belgian coast (pop. 32,000) has several districts, all with their own character.

Heist used to be a fishing village, Duinbergen attracted painters and poets associated with Symbolism, and Knokke was home to polder farmers. Het Zoute, the most exclusive part, is a garden town with stately villas owned by the Brussels and Antwerp elite – which is why the language here is almost exclusively French, and why the long *Kustlaan* is a shopping street of luxury boutiques, fancy antique dealers and expensive art galleries.

SIGHTSEEING

ALBERTPLEIN
The Brussels chic set regularly turns the *Place m'as-tu-vu* ('Boaster Square') in the Het Zoute part of town into a proper fashion and car show.

CASINO
It was René Magritte himself who adorned the casino with his 72m/236-ft-long wall painting 'Le Domaine enchanté'. Also on view: paintings by Paul Delvaux, Constant Permeke and Léon Spilliaert. Any visits have to take place as part of a guided tour organised by Toer-

isme Knokke. *Daily from 3pm | Zeedijk-Albertstrand 509*

RUBENSPLEIN ⌇
This square was given an avant-garde makeover by the Belgian star architects Robbrecht & Daem and the Austrian artist Franz West. *Albertstrand*

VILLA NOORDHINDER/WESTHINDER
Henry van de Velde built these villas in 1930 in the Bauhaus style. *Zeedijk-Het Zoute 219–220*

Architectural imagination is much in evidence at the Rubensplein square in Knokke-Heist

FOOD & DRINK

BARTHOLOMEUS ⌇
The imaginative menu features delicious fish and meat dishes. Fine sea views too. *Closed Tue–Thu | Zeedijk 267 | tel. 050 51 75 76 | www.restaurantbartholomeus. be | Expensive*

KNOKKE-HEIST

BEL-ETAGE
Intimate restaurant in an traditional house, imaginative seasonal cuisine. *Closed Wed and at lunchtime | Guldenvliesstraat 13 | tel. 050 62 77 33 | www.bel-etage.be |* *Expensive*

PANIER D'OR
Modern brasserie with terrace. Good fish dishes, and there are children's menus too. *Closed Tue | Zeedijk-Heist 659 | tel. 050 60 31 89 |* *Budget*

the 158 ha nature reserve, and countless migratory species take a well-earned rest. *Natuurreservaat Het Zwin | Easter–30 Sept Tue–Sun 9am–5.30pm, Oct–Easter 9am-4.30pm, during the Belgian school holidays Mon too | admission 5.20 euros | Graaf Léon Lippensdreef 8 | www.zwin.be*

ZWINBOSJES
Well signposted cycle and hiking paths can be found east of Het Zoute in 220 ha of protected forested dunes, seamlessly giving way to extensive polder country.

The Het Zwin nature reserve is ideal territory for hiking and birdwatching

SPORTS & ACTIVITIES

BEACH CLUB HEIST
Central hub for all kinds of water sports. Courses, equipment hire. *Zeedijk-Heist 197 | www.vvwheist.be*

HET ZWIN
The Zwin is perfect for hikers and bird-watchers: over 120 bird species breed in

BEACHES

The end of the Zwinlaan in *Het Zoute* marks the beginning of a broad sandy beach 4 km/2.5 miles long, only fringed by sea, sky and dunes. The beach of Het Zoute features exclusive clubs, while family life reigns in *Albertstrand*, *Duinbergen* and *Heist*.

WHERE TO STAY

MANOIR DU DRAGON
Country house built in 1927 and set in extensive gardens. Luxurious rooms with terrace/balcony and garden views. Fabulous breakfast. *15 rooms | Albertlaan 73 | tel. 050 63 05 80 | www.manoirdu dragon.be | Expensive*

LA RÉSERVE
This new luxury hotel occupies an exclusive location on Zegemeer Lake. Ilse De Meulemeester styled the opulent interior using plenty of black, gold and turquoise and sparing no expense. Elegant bar and gourmet restaurant *Dinners 160,* light-filled bistro with lake views, Knokke's only ballroom and most of all the ● ⋇ spa on the 6th floor with a stunning, relaxing panoramic view of sea and sky from the pool and relaxation room. *110 rooms | Elizabetlaan 160 | tel. 050 61 06 06 | www.la-reserve.be | Expensive*

HOTEL TER HEIS ⋇
Basic yet keenly priced hotel – right by the beach, with its own terrace and situated in front of the sailing club. *20 rooms | Zeedijk 210 | tel. 050 51 78 84 | www.beachhotelsknokkeheist.be | Budget*

INFORMATION

Dienst Toerisme | Zeedijk-Heist 660 | tel. 050 63 03 80 | www.knokke-heist.be

WHERE TO GO

BLANKENBERGE (124 C1) (*∅ D3*)
Blankenberge (pop. 17,000, 8 km/5 miles west of Knokke-Heist), is the most popular, down-to-earth resort. The sea promenade is a bit of a fun fair, and the packed beach is used for picnics. The pier juts out into the sea for 350 m/over 380 yards. Its far end features a ⋇ restaurant with views into infinity and a model railway exhibition. The *Paravang*, a long windbreak at the marina, is a gem of Art Nouveau style with benches for sunbathing, people-watching and chatting. *Information: Dienst Toerisme | Leopold-III-plein | tel. 050 41 22 27 | www. blankenberge.be*

DE HAAN (124 C2) (*∅ C3*)
Genteel resort 17 km/10 miles southwest of Knokke-Heist. Extensive dunes and polder marshes frame the little town of villas (pop. 10,000), where the charm of the Belle Époque has survived. You'll find a quiet wide sandy beach, and to the west, on the border with Bredene, the **INSIDER TIP** only nudist beach on the coast. Four riding stables hire out horses for treks through dunes and forests. Hikers and cycling folk also love De Haan and its surroundings. For classy accommodation within a large garden and a pool, choose the *Romantik Manoir Carpe Diem hotel (16 rooms | tel. 059 23 32 20 | www.manoircarpediem.com | Prins Karellaan 12 | Expensive).* For a nice bed & breakfast, try *Villa Stella Maris (3 rooms | Memlinglaan 11 | tel. 059 23 56 69 | www. stellamaris.be | Budget). Information: Dienst Toerisme | Leopoldlaan 24 | tel. 059 24 21 34 | www.dehaan.be*

KORTRIJK

(125 D5) (*∅ D–E7*) Kortrijk (pop. 76,000) has no scruples about flaunting its nouveau-riche wealth. Ladies dressed to kill speed to terminally chic boutiques in luxury cars.
What is behind this wealth is evident in Kortrijk's surroundings, where countless factories produce carpets, industrial textiles and design furniture. Every other

year the renowned *Biennale Interieur* brings together the best designers. The shopping paradise centres around the huge *K* shopping mall designed by Paul Robbrecht and Hilde Daem in Kortrijk, between Veemarkt and Steenstraat.

SIGHTSEEING

BEGIJNHOF
Fairy-tale village with cobbled lanes, white-washed cottages and gardens full of flowers. *Sint-Maartenskerkhof*

BROELMUSEUM
An elegant 18th-century patrician palace, showing works by Roelant Savery, the Kortrijk-born court painter of Emperor Rudolph II in Prague, but also 19th-century landscapes. The orangery houses a classy cafeteria. *Tue–Fri 10am–12 noon and 2–5pm, Sat/Sun 11am–5pm | admission 3 euros | Broelkaai 6*

GROTE MARKT
The playful belfry with glockenspiel occupies a lone position on the square. Another eye-catcher is the richly adorned late Gothic town hall.

NATIONAAL VLAS-, KANT- EN -LINNENMUSEUM
The National Museum dedicated to flax, lace and linen covers all aspects of these traditional Kortrijk products. *Tue–Fri 9am–12.30pm and 1.30–6pm, Sat/Sun 2–6pm | admission 3 euros | Etienne Sabbelaan 4*

ONZE-LIEVE-VROUWEKERK
The ducal chapel of this Gothic church is home to masterly portraits of all dukes of Flanders. Particularly worth seeing are 'Saint Catharine of Alexandria' created around 1380 by sculptor André Beauneveu and the 'Raising of the Cross' by Anthony van Dyck. *Corner Onze-Lieve-Vrouwestraat/Begijnhofstraat*

FOOD & DRINK

TABLE D'AMIS ☺
Matthieu Beudaert prepares modern light interpretations of regional dishes in his own elegant home, always using seasonal local produce. *Closed Mon/Tue and Sat lunchtime | Walle 184 | tel. 056 32 82 70 | www.tabledamis.be | Moderate–Expensive*

WHERE TO STAY

INSIDER TIP D-HOTEL
Cool and stylish design hotel on the edge of town, with high-tech facilities, spa, fabulous artist-designed suites and a hip bistro. *45 rooms | Abdijmolenweg 1 | tel. 056 21 21 00 | www.d-hotel.be | Moderate*

DAMIER
Traditional establishment on the market square with classy rooms. Belle Époque brasserie, elegant gourmet restaurant. *49 rooms | Grote Markt 41 | tel. 056 22 15 47 | www.hoteldamier.be | Moderate*

INFORMATION
Toerisme Kortrijk | Schouwburgplein 14a | tel. 056 27 78 40 | www.kortrijk.be

WHERE TO GO

IEPER (124 B5) (*ɷ B7*)
In 1914, Ieper (Ypres, pop. 35,000) was razed to the ground by the Germans. A million soldiers died in the area and are commemorated by the Memorial Arch of Ypres, 16 km/10 miles west of Kortrijk. Other moving memorials are the sublime ● *Menenpoort* gate where the Last Post is played every evening, and the

St George's Memorial Church. In the monumental ⭐ *Lakenhal* with ☀ belfry, one of the most sublime secular Gothic buildings in the world, the *In Flanders' Fields Museum (April–Oct daily 10am–6pm, Nov–March Tue–Sun 10am–5pm | admission 8 euros, belfry an additional 2 euros | Grote Markt 32 | www.inflanders fields.be)* presents impressive audio and film documents from the First World War. *Information: Toerisme Ieper | Grote Markt 34 | tel. 057 23 92 20 | www.ieper.be*

seum | March, Nov Tue–Fri 10am–6pm, Sat/Sun 2–6pm | admission 5 euros | Gasthuisstraat 71)* will appeal to lovers of good ale. Every year, *Watou* village, now part of the town, hosts the *Poetry and Arts Festival (July/Aug | www.kunstenfestivalwatou.be)*. The best beer around, *Westvleteren,* is brewed by the Trappists

The Lakenhal with belfry in Ypres – the most opulent of all the Flemish cloth halls

POPERINGE (124 B5) (🗺 *A–B 6–7*)
In Poperinge (pop. 19,500, 32 km/20 miles west of Kortrijk), three Gothic churches are testimonies to the former wealth of the town, based on cloth manufacture. Flax and hops grow in the fields around. Dedicated to the plant used to flavour beer, the *Hops Museum (hop mu-*

in their *Sint-Sixtus Abbey.* As the monks sold the recipes shortly after the Second World War, the beers of the Sint-Bernardus micro-brewery in Watou are identical – and much easier to obtain.

For quiet accommodation try the *Hotel Recour (8 rooms | Guido Gezellestraat 7 | tel. 057 33 57 25 | www.pegasusrecour.be | Expensive)* with its gourmet restaurant *Pegasus. Information: Toerisme Poperinge | Grote Markt 1 | tel. 057 34 66 76 | www.poperinge.be*

OOSTENDE

(124 B2) *(ω B–C 3–4)* **This city of 69,000 inhabitants carries on living when the holiday guests have gone home again. In the Belle Époque, Oostende was one of Europe's most chic resorts.**

King Leopold II use Oostende as his summer residence, paying for ornate buildings and the purchase of dunes out of his

KONINKLIJKE GAANDEREIEN ● ⅍

King Leopold II had the 400m/440-yard arcades built to allow him to proceed from his villa to the racetrack in the shade. Even on a rainy day it makes for an atmospheric stroll with views of the empty beach and the grey sea. *Zeedijk*

MERCATOR

Sailing ship formerly used for training in the merchant navy. *April–June, Sept daily*

Port of Oostende: the resort was already a popular holiday destination in the Belle Époque era

own pocket. The town suffered greatly in both the First and the Second World Wars.

SIGHTSEEING

JAMES ENSORHUIS

The famous painter James Ensor lived here between 1917 and 1949. His monumental masterpiece 'Christ's Entry in Brussels' used to hang in the sitting room; today it has been replaced by a reproduction. *Wed–Mon 10am–12 noon and 2–5pm | admission 2 euros | Vlaanderenstraat 27*

10am–12.30pm and 2–5.30pm, July/Aug daily 10am–5.30pm, Oct–March Sat/Sun and school holidays 10am–12.30pm and 2–4.30pm | admission 4 euros | Mercatordok

MU.ZEE

In a converted warehouse, the museum for modern art of West Flanders province shows Belgian art of the 19th and 20th centuries and puts on outstanding exhibitions. *Tue–Sun 10am–6pm | admission 5 euros | Romestraat 11 | www.muzee.be*

STAKETSEL ⚡
Jutting out 600m/650yd into the sea, the western jetty is popular for strolls, at sunset in particular. *Montgomerykaai*

VISTRAP
The old fish market has stalls selling delicious fishy snacks. *Visserskaai*

FOOD & DRINK

FORT NAPOLEON
Cool stylish restaurant in a massive fort in the dunes, serving light seasonal dishes, also on its pleasant terrace. *Closed Mon | Vuurtorenweg | tel. 059 33 21 60 | www. fortnapoleon.be | Expensive*

MATHILDA
Brasserie serving fish and meat dishes, equipped with an enormous counter for taking an aperitif. *Closed Mon/Tue | Leopold-II-laan 1 | tel. 059 51 06 70 | www. bistromathilda.be | Budget*

OSTEND QUEEN ⚡
Star chef Pierre Wynants' fish brasserie has a location above the casino. Mega-chic design, and the lounge is a meeting place for the top set. However, you'll still find the traditional speciality here: INSIDER TIP *Smeus*, a potato-vegetable-pap with seafood. The cold seafood platter has to be seen to be believed. Elegant attire is required, as is a reservation! *Closed Tue/Wed | Monacoplein (entrance Westhelling) | tel. 059 44 56 10 | www. ostendqueen.be | Moderate*

BEACHES

FORT NAPOLEON
Quiet beach east of the harbour pier, below the fort. The *Blue Link* barge *(departures daily 10am–6pm | Sir Winston Churchillkaai | single ticket 1.50 euros,* bike 0.50 euros) takes five minutes to cross the harbour.

ZEEDIJK
The most popular hence busiest beach in the centre of Oostende extends in front of the elegant Royal Arcades.

WHERE TO STAY

Holiday apartments along the entire coast can be rented through *www.dermul. be* and *www.lacotebelge.be*, amongst others. *www.belvilla.de* specialises in holiday villas and bungalows.

HOTEL 'T KRUISHOF
Farm on the edge of town, with garden, sun terrace, tennis, playground. Nice rooms and generous breakfast. *11 rooms | Kruishofstraat 1 | tel. 059 70 98 44 | www.kruishof.be | Budget*

ROYAL ALBERT
Pretty rooms with views of the sea and an in-house traditional restaurant. *22*

LOW BUDGET

▶ The *Brugge City Card (35 euros for 48 hours, 40 euros for 72 hours | www.bruggecitycard.be and from Toerisme Brugge)* allows free admission to 26 sights, one free boat tour round the canals and a 25 per cent discount for cultural events, bike hire and in multi-storey car parks.

▶ Oostende offers a *City Pass (12 euros for 24 hours, 20 euros for 72 hours | available from Toerisme Oostende)* giving access to all important sights.

rooms | Zeedijk 167 | tel. 059 70 42 36 | users.skynet.be/royal.albert | Budget

THERMAE PALACE
Splendid hotel in Art Deco style with generously sized rooms, a bistro and an elegant gourmet restaurant. *156 rooms | Koningin Astridlaan 7 | tel. 059 80 66 44 | www.thermaepalace.be | Expensive*

INFORMATION

Toerisme Oostende | Monacoplein 2 | tel. 059 70 11 99 | www.toerisme-oostende.be

WHERE TO GO

DE PANNE (124 A3) *(m A4–5)*
Sand yachts, windsurfers and kitesurfers populate the vast beach of this modern resort (pop. 9500); to the west, the dunes of the 350 ha *Westhoek* nature reserve continue into France. Cycle paths, riding and hiking trails lead all the way into the polder terrain. *Information: Dienst Toerisme | Zeelaan 21 | tel. 058 42 18 18 | www.depanne.be*

KOKSIJDE (124 A3) *(m A4)*
This resort (pop. 19,000) with its fine broad beaches lies 28 km/17 miles southwest of Oostende. The ruins of the once-wealthy *Ten Duinen Cistercian abbey* are worth seeing. In the Sint-Idesbald part of town, the Surrealist painter Paul Delvaux donated masterpieces and a *museum (April–Sept Tue–Sun, Oct–Dec Thu–Sun 10.30am–5.30pm | admission 8 euros | Paul Delvauxlaan 5).* The ● *Nationaal Visserijmuseum (Tue–Fri 10am–6pm, Sat/Sun*

BOOKS & FILMS

▶ **Brothers** – (2000) Children's book author Bart Moeyaert remembers his happy-go-lucky childhood in Flanders

▶ **The Sorrow of Belgium** – (1983) In this masterful family epic, Hugo Claus settles some scores with the Catholic fascist petite bourgeoisie in the West Flemish province in the years 1930–50

▶ **My Fellow Skin** – (2000) Erwin Mortier describes the social rise of the Flemish in the decades of 1955–75 through the eyes of an adolescent

▶ **The Midas Murders** – (1996) Like all murder mysteries by Pieter Aspe, this too is set in Bruges, featuring the beer-loving Inspector Pieter Van In and an attractive prosecutor

▶ **Sleep!** – (2003) In her debut novel, Annelies Verbeke follows a woman with insomnia on her wanderings through Antwerp

▶ **Ben X** – (2007) Nic Balthazar gained world-wide success with his gripping film about an autistic boy made on location in Flanders

▶ **Bruges** – (2008) Blend of thriller and comedy by Martin McDonagh, featuring stars such as Colin Farrell and Ralph Fiennes. The starring role went to the film's location Bruges

▶ **Cut Loose** – (2008) Director Jan Verheyen delves into progressive Flanders, which abhors racism and is in favour of euthanasia. The backdrop is Antwerp

2–6pm | admission 5 euros | Pastoor Schmitzstraat 5 | www.visserijmuseum.be) is a good source of information on fishing, have come to the right place here. *Information: Dienst Toerisme | Marktplein 7 | tel. 058 22 44 44 | www.nieuwpoort.be*

Cosy frame for a fine square: step-gabled houses on Grote Markt in Veurne

prawn fishing in particular. In the Oostduinkerke part of town, the fishermen still head out into the mudflats with their horses on a near-daily basis *(www.paardenvissers.be)*. In the quiet neighbourhood around the Delvaux-Museum you'll find the *Villa Certi Momenti (3 rooms | Myriamweg 16 | tel. 058 51 89 05 | www.certimomenti.be | Budget)* with sun terrace. *Information: Dienst Toerisme | Leopold-II-laan 2 | tel. 058 53 21 21 | www.koksijde.be*

NIEUWPOORT (124 B3) (*𝄃 B4*)

This town of 9000 inhabitants on the Ijzer estuary, 17 km/10.5 miles southwest of Oostende, was completely destroyed in the two world wars. The *town hall,* the *cloth hall* with belfry and the *Church of Our Lady* were rebuilt in 1925 and 1950. Today Nieuwpoort attracts many water sports aficionados with a marina and excellent sailing schools. Kayakers, windsurfers, kitesurfers and divers as well as fans of waterskiing and wavekarting

VEURNE ⭐ (124 A3) (*𝄃 A5*)

This similarly sized tranquil town (pop. 8500, 25 km/15 miles to the southwest) is dominated by the bulky tower of the Gothic *Sint-Niklaaskerk*. The *Grote Markt* enchants with cheerful stepped gable houses. The *town hall* and the so-called *Landhaus (April–Sept daily 11am, 2pm, 3pm, 4.30pm, Oct–March daily 11am and 3pm | free admission)* with its elegant belfry and lavishly decorated halls date back to Renaissance times. *Information: Dienst Toerisme | Grote Markt 29 | tel. 058 33 55 31 | www.veurne.be*

VLADSLO ⭐ (124 B3) (*𝄃 C5*)

The German war cemetery, 16 km/10 miles south of Oostende, shelters the remains of over 25,000 soldiers who lost their lives here in World War I. Watching over the granite slabs are the 'Mourning Parents' by sculptor Käthe Kollwitz. *Daily 9am–6pm*

GHENT AND EAST FLANDERS

Sublime architecture, masterpieces of art, flowing landscapes and heavenly tranquillity characterise the province of East Flanders, with the old ducal town of Ghent at its centre.

Waterways radiate from here like a spider's web, rivers with many bends and old channels such as the Schelde or Leie, straight canals heading in all directions, flanked by poplars and willows, fields and pastures.

The polders of Meetjesland in the northwest, on the border to the Netherlands, are amongst the most picturesque corners of East Flanders. On the eastern edge of the province, the Demer river makes its way through the landscape. In the south the Flemish Ardennes present a completely different picture: this chain of hills some 150 m/500 feet high is well-known to racing cyclists. Garden designers and amateur gardeners too know this province: azaleas and begonias of world renown are grown at Lochristi and Beervelde, east of Ghent.

GHENT

MAP INSIDE BACK COVER
(125 F3–4) (*M G5*) **Ghent (pop. 224,000) receives its visitors with the vibrant buzz of an old university city – 65,000 students stroll, discuss and enjoy the nightlife.**

In the region, only Ghent can rival Antwerp for varied nightlife and a real cultural scene. As a backdrop to this, impres-

Photo: Graslei in Gent

Rivers, canals and hills even: the attractions of old Ghent include culture and vibrant life, complemented by the nature and dolce vita of its surroundings

CITY

WHERE TO START?

Sint-Michielsbrug: this bridge spanning the Leie makes an ideal starting point. Close by you have Sint-Niklaaskerk, belfry and cathedral, Graslei, Korenlei and Gravensteen, as well as the shopping districts. Drivers follow the P-Route to the multi-storey car parks P7 Sint-Michiels or P9 Belfort, train travellers take tram 1 (direction of Evergem) to Korenmarkt.

sive monuments put the spotlight on the history of Flanders.

Ghent was once one of Europe's wealthiest cloth-weaving towns in Europe, with citizens and guilds that were well aware of their status. Thus in 1540, Ghent faced down Emperor Charles V, when he tried to levy a new war tax on his people. When the textile industry blossomed again in the 19th century, this was where the Flemish workers' movement started. Today, Ghent is a place of beauty. The Lieve and Leie flow into the Schelde here,

Bulwark of grey stone: the Gravensteen moated castle

BELFORT ⚜

Rising in the centre of the expansive space between cathedral and the Old Post Office, the medieval belfry was built between 1313 and 1380 and illustrates the power of the town's patricians and guilds. On the second floor of the very small cloth hall, to this day the exclusive royal guild of Saint Michael's founded in 1613, still practices foil fencing. The tower with glockenspiel offers fine panoramic views. Between belfry and cathedral the architects Paul Robbrecht and Hilde Daem built an avant-garde interpretation of a hall and forum – a new, fairly controversial landmark. *March–Nov daily 10am–6pm | admission 5 euros | Sint-Baafsplein*

BOEKENTOREN

This 64 m/210-ft modern icon was designed by Henry van de Velde in 1933 for the University Library and dominates the city from the Blandijnberg elevation. *Rozier 9*

DESIGN MUSEUM

The De Coninck Rococo palace shows precious antique furniture. The new museum has an extensive collection of Art Nouveau furniture and objects, as well as contemporary design. The works by Flemish designer Pieter De Bruyne, pioneer of the Italian Transavanguardia movement, are quite an eyecatcher. *Tue–Sun 10am–6pm | admission 5 euros | Jan Breydelstraat 5 | design.museum.gent.be*

GRASLEI AND KORENLEI

Ghent's two faces are reflected in the water of the first harbour: plain medieval stepped gables of warehouses and guild's quarters of Lager-Graslei, cheerful Baroque façades along the Korenlei. It's

and are connected by canals. Tree-lined waterfronts offer plenty of opportunity to stroll and allow the city's variety to work its magic on you. Between sunset and midnight the INSIDERTIP city centre is illuminated like a fairy-tale, and during the Festival of Lights in January, designers and artists use the façades to create breath-taking effects.

worth strolling on a bit further – to the north, Ghent remains a bit austere *(Kraanlei, Oudburg)*, keeping its elegant side to the south *(Recollettenlei, Lindenlei, Coupure)*.

GRAVENSTEEN ⭐

Around the year 1000, the dukes of Flanders started building a moated castle from grey Schelde stone. Over the course of two centuries, the symbol of their power and their 24 towers rose, with the hall and a 30 m/ 100-ft ceiling at its centre. Later on the castle was to serve as court, torture chamber for the Inquisition and a cotton spinning mill. Old court documents, weapons and implements of torture illustrate the castle's former incarnations. *April–Sept daily 9am–6pm, Oct–March daily 9am–5pm | admission 8 euros | Sint-Veerleplein*

MIAT

Housed in a former cotton spinning mill, the museum for industrial archaeology and textile technology gives an idea of day-to-day working life in the era between 1750 and 2000. The cafeteria with views of the gardens provides a welcome break. *Tue–Sun 10am–6pm | admission 5 euros | Minnemeers 9 | www.miat.gent.be*

INSIDER TIP ▶ MUSEUM DR GUISLAIN

Jozef Guislain was one of the founders of modern, humane psychiatry, as you can see by the architecture of his clinic in Ghent. The museum illustrates the history of psychiatry and stages excellent exhibitions of art brut. *Tue–Fri 9am–5pm, Sat/Sun 1–5pm | admission 6 euros | Jozef Guislainstraat 43 | Tram 1 | www.museum drguislain.be*

MUSEUM VOOR SCHONE KUNSTEN

A Neoclassical building forms a sublime shrine to high-quality art from the Middle Ages to around 1950. Visitors come for the collection of French painters and German Expressionists. Amongst the highlights are 'The Crucifixion' by Hieronymus Bosch and the 'Portrait of a Kleptomaniac' by Théodore Géricault. The museum is particularly strong on the Flemish Impressionists and Expressionists of the Sint-Martens-Latem school. One instructive room is devoted to the social conditions of 19th century workers and peasants. *Tue–Sun 10am–6pm | admission 5 euros | Fernand Scribedreef 1 (Citadel Park) | www.msk gent.be*

MARCO POLO HIGHLIGHTS

⭐ **Gravensteen**
The dukes of Flanders' awe-inspiring moated castle in Ghent
→ p. 51

⭐ **Sint-Baafskathedraal**
Gothic and Baroque styles, plus the masterful Ghent Altarpiece
→ p. 52

⭐ **S.M.A.K.**
To discover Flanders' leading museum showcasing the artistic avant-garde of yesterday and today, head for Ghent
→ p. 53

⭐ **Stadhuis**
Stylistic diversity illustrates the wealth of the proud city of Ghent → p. 53

⭐ **Centrum Ronde van Vlaanderen**
In Oudenaarde, the legendary tours of Flemish racing cyclists are presented as if you were right there with them → p. 57

SINT-BAAFSKATHEDRAAL ⭐

Ghent's cathedral unites several styles. Choir and transept were built in the clear style of Schelde Gothic, while the aisled nave and the tower are typical of the more playful style of Brabant Gothic. The mix of red brick, grey Schelde stone and French limestone creates an astonishing effect. The impressive Baroque interior was added after the devastation wrought

5pm, Sun 1–5pm, Nov–March Mon–Sat 10.30am–4pm, Sun 1–4pm (admission 4 euros) | free admission | Sint-Baafsplein

SINT-NIKLAASKERK

Dedicated to St Nicholas, this church of Schelde stone with its clear lines is among the most beautiful examples of Schelde Gothic. The view inside the tower its fascinating. The monumental Roman-

Ghent high up: from Sint-Baafskathedraal you have far-ranging views across the city

by the wars of religion. The cathedral is world-famous for its ● *Ghent Altarpiece* by Jan and Hubert van Eyck. The central panel shows the 'Adoration of the Mystic Lamb'. Stolen several times over, this masterpiece of old Dutch painting is now kept behind bullet-proof glass in the baptismal chapel. The panels are being restored one by one over the coming years in the Museum voor Schone Kunsten; visitors are allowed to watch the specialists at work. *Cathedral April–Oct daily 8.30am–6pm, Nov–March daily 8.30am–5pm, Ghent Altarpiece April–Oct Mon–Sat 9.30am–*

tic Cavaillé-Coll organ (1856) was recently restored as part of the overall restoration work. It is possible to listen to INSIDER TIP **professors and students of the musical college playing,** as the Flentrop organ in the choir is used for teaching. *Mon 2–5pm, Tue–Sun 10am–5pm | admission free | Cataloniestraat*

SINT-PIETERSABDIJ

The splendid Baroque church is a reminder of the wealth of the former Benedictine abbey, and is used for exhibitions today. Behind the abbey, discover an ● oasis of peace and tranquillity with a herbal garden, a meadow full of apple trees and even a vineyard *(access through gate and courtyard Sint-Pietersplein 12 noon–3pm). Tue–Sun 10am–6pm | free admission | Sint-Pietersplein 9 | www.sintpietersabdij gent.be*

S.M.A.K. ★

The Municipal Museum for Contemporary Art owes its fame to its long-serving director Jan Hoet, who put together a fascinating collection (featuring Marcel Broodthaers, Joseph Beuys, and Luc Tuymans, amongst others) with the help of artists and patrons. Excellent exhibitions, and the popular artists' café stays open till 1am. *Tue–Sun 10am–6pm | admission 6 euros | Citadel Park | www.smak.be*

STADHUIS ★

The Town Hall was built in the Late Gothic, Renaissance and Baroque periods. Rather than dominating a square it occupies a democratic position at two street corners. Inside, splendid halls are a testimony to the power and wealth of the town. *May–Oct Mon–Thu 2.30pm (advance reservation 11am–2pm through the Dienst Toerisme) | admission 6 euros | Botermarkt 1*

STAM

In this medieval *Bijloke Monastery and Hospice* Ghent's history unfolds through showpiece examples of local craft work. The former hospital room with its unique beams is used as a concert hall. *Tue–Sun 10am–6pm | admission 6 euros | Godshuizenlaan 2 | www.stamgent.be*

VRIJDAGMARKT

The market was often the scene of riots, demonstrations and strike events. *Ons Huis (no. 9–10)*, built in a curious eclectic style, is the house of the socialist trade union.

ZUID

For the World Exhibition of 1913, Ghent spruced itself up to embrace modernity. The splendid INSIDERTIP *Sint-Pieters railway station* by Louis Cloquet in the Zuid district is a fascinating example of early Art Deco, the neighbourhoods to the north and south boast many Art Nouveau and Art Deco houses.

FOOD & DRINK

INSIDERTIP BORD'EAU ☺

Trendy styled brasserie in the old fish market hall, a fine bar and a fabulous terrace on the water. The menu features unusual Ghent dishes and ingredients. *Closed Sun evening | Sint-Veerleplein 5 | tel. 09 22 32 00 | www.oudevismijn.be | Budget*

INSIDERTIP CAFÉ THÉÂTRE

Elegant mix of café, brasserie and lounge in the opera house. At weekends disco

LOW BUDGET

▶ For friendly, excellent-value bed & breakfasts check out *www.bedandbreakfast-gent.be.*

▶ In the months of June to September, Ghent University rents out 340 rooms in student halls of residence. *Tel. 09 2 64 71 00 | www.use-it.be*

▶ The *Museum Pass* for museums, Gravensteen Castle, belfry and the Ghent Altarpiece makes sense, allowing visitors to take bus and trams for free, for three days running. *20 euros | available from the museums and the Dienst Toerisme*

GHENT

with DJs for hip parties. *Closed Sat lunchtime | Schouwburgstraat 5 | tel. 09 2 65 05 50 | www.cafetheatre.be | Moderate*

INSIDER TIP GRUUT

This microbrewery uses a secret mix of herbs to flavour its special brews, and serves an interesting elderflower aperitif called *Roomer*. Great vibes within the industrial-chic walls and on the terrace. *Mon–Wed 11am–6pm, Thu–Sat 11am–midnight, Sun 2–7pm | Grote Huidevettershoek 21 | www.gruut.be*

J.E.F. ☺

Flemish Foodie Jason Blanckaert doesn't shy away from risqué combinations using local produce. Fine beer list. On Fridays from 10pm they put on a cool INSIDER TIP after-work party with unusual finger food. Trendy clientele. *Closed Sun/Mon | Lange Steenstraat 10 | tel. 09 3 36 80 58 | www.j-e-f.be | Budget–Moderate*

PAKHUIS

Plenty of good vibes, excellent food and friendly service in a spectacular warehouse. More intimate café section. *Closed Sun | Schuurkenstraat 4 | tel. 09 2 23 55 55 | Budget*

SHOPPING

In and around *Veldstraat* the chain stores rule, while chic boutiques await in *Kalandeberg, Koestraat, Kortedagsteeg* and *Walpoortstraat.*
Around *Onderbergen* you'll find fine antiques and design shops, and the *flea market (Fri–Sun 8am–1pm)* around Sint-Jacob's Church. On *Kortrijksepoortstraat* and *Dampoortstraat* are many second-hand shops.

BAKKERIJ IMSCHOOT

Traditional bakery selling specialties such as the *Gentse Mokken* and *Kletskoppen* cookies, as well as honey and spiced cake. *Groentenmarkt 1*

VITS-STAELENS

Sage and elderflower syrups, Ghent genever, liqueurs. *Bij Sint Jacobs 14*

VVE. TIERENTYN-VERLENT

This is where top chefs buy their fiery mustards – a legend since 1790. *Groentenmarkt 3*

INSIDER TIP YUZU

Sold in a Japanese-inspired austere ambience: exquisite chocolates with a jasmine, tea or citrus filling. *Walpoortstraat 11a*

VEGGIEDAG GENT

In May 2009, Ghent make international headlines, when the city announced Thursdays to be 'Veggiedays'. Creches and canteens would not serve meat or fish, good news for the climate, health and purse. Hasselt, Mechelen and Sint-Niklaas, as well as Washington DC – and UK Meat-Free Mondays – followed the good example. In Ghent meanwhile, things have moved one step further, as the city encourages its residents to drink tap water instead of mineral water from PET bottles. *www.donderdagveggiedag.be* lists all restaurants, snack bars and even frites stalls that promote the trend, as well as tasty recipes.

BOAT TRIP

Why not hire a small motorboat to chug along the Leie River in Ghent and surroundings. *MBC | from 53 euros | Minerva-Haven, corner Coupure right/Lindelaan 2a | tel. 09 2337917 | www.minervaboten.be*

train station, direction of Moscou | single ticket 1.20 euros from the ticket machine

ENTERTAINMENT

Night owls will feel right at home in Ghent. Cafés and clubs frequented by the student population cluster in *Overpoortstraat,* while a mixed clientele hits the

Shopping expedition in Ghent: welcome refreshments in street cafés

POOL

Flanders' oldest indoor swimming pool is a treat for all fans of Art Deco, which makes backstroke the favourite option for sightseeing. *Zwembad Van Eyck | Veermanplein 1 | Opening times at www.gent.be/sport | admission 5 euros*

TRAM TOUR

To get an impression of various neighbourhoods of Ghent and their inhabitants, take tram no. 4, which passes through outlying districts to reach the historic centre and then goes on to other outlying districts. *Departures from the Sint-Pieters*

clubs at *Vlasmarkt*. The *Zuid district* is on the up right now. For a quieter night, head for the *Patershol* neighbourhood (near Gravensteen Castle).

CHARLATAN

Buzzing venue where the party goes on till after dawn. Regular free live concerts. Quieter cocktail bar next door (Tue–Sat 4pm–4am). *Tue–Sun from 9pm | Vlasmarkt 6 | www.charlatan.be*

CLUB CENTRAL

This club has tango and salsa playing on the ground floor, pop music in the cellar vaults. *Tue–Sun from 8pm onwards | Hoogport 32 | www.clubcentral.be*

HOPDUVEL

Cosy beer garden attached to a microbrewery, serving an appropriately broad selection of the good stuff. *Rokerelstraat 10*

INSIDERTIP JIGGER'S

In a saloon-bar ambiance Olivier Jacobs mixes exciting cocktails – involving genever from Ghent – which won Belgian and European competitions. *Mon–Thu 5pm–1am, Fri/Sat 5pm–2.30am | Oudburg 16 | www.jiggers.be*

KINKY STAR

Disco run by the record label of the same name; this is where the best DJs in town spin their tunes. *Tue–Sun 8pm–5am | Vlasmarkt 9 | www.kinkystar.com*

VOORUIT

The Art Nouveau halls are today used by the socialist workers movement to put on avant-garde dance, theatre and music for a studenty clientele. Smoke-filled café. *Sint-Pietersnieuwstraat 23 | tel. 09 2 67 28 28 | www.vooruit.be*

WHERE TO STAY

INSIDERTIP ECOHOSTEL ANDROMEDA ☺

From insulation via the bed linen and water filtering to the organic breakfast: this converted freight barge on a quiet canal has 100 per cent sound eco credentials. *2 doubles and 2 rooms sleeping 6 and 8 | Bargiekaai 35 | tel. mobil 0486 67 80 33 | www.ecohostel.be | Budget*

HOTEL ERASMUS

Two old patrician houses with a friendly atmosphere and a well-kept garden. *11 rooms | Poel 25 | tel. 09 2 24 21 95 | www.erasmushotel.be | Moderate*

HOTEL GRAVENSTEEN

Elegant hotel in a classy patrician palace. Some rooms with a view of the ducal castle, others with a view of the quiet garden. *49 rooms | Jan Breydelstraat 35 | tel. 09 2 25 11 50 | www.gravensteen.be | Expensive*

MONASTERIUM POORTACKERE

This former monastery offers the option of guest rooms in former cells – not exactly en-suite but atmospheric for sure. *45 rooms and 13 cells | Oude Houtlei 56 | tel. 09 2 69 22 10 | www.monasterium. be | Budget–Moderate*

INFORMATION

Dienst Toerisme | Sint-Veerleplein 5 | tel. 09 2 66 56 60 | www.visitgent.be

WHERE TO GO

KASTEEL OOIDONK (125 E4) (*Ø F5*)

The impressive Renaissance moated castle, still inhabited by its ducal owners, lies only 5km/3 miles southwest of Ghent. *April–June and Sept Sun 2–5.30pm, July/Aug Sat/Sun 2–5.30 | admission 7 euros | Ooidonkdreef 9 | Bachte-Maria-Leie | www.ooidonk.be*

OUDENAARDE (125 E5) (*Ø F7*)

This small town (pop. 27,500) on the Schelde, 28 km/17 miles south of Ghent is famous for its tapestries dating from the 16–18th centuries. These depictions of landscapes, called *verdures*, were sought-after all over Europe. Beautiful specimens can be found hanging in the late Gothic town hall *(April–Oct Mon–Fri 11am and 3pm, Sat/Sun 2 and 4pm, only with guided tour | admission 5 euros)*, a treasure trove on the large market square.

With its severe lines, the *Onze-Lieve-Vrouw-van-Pamele* church on the right bank of the Schelde is one of the most beautiful examples of Schelde Gothic. The ⭐ ● *Centrum Ronde van Vlaanderen (Tue–Sun 10am–6pm | admission 8 euros | Markt 43 | www.crvv.be)* whisks visitors away into the mythic world of the *flandriens,* Flemish racing cyclists (excellent museum gift shop). Next to the town hall you'll find the hotel and restaurant *Hostellerie La*

Symbolist sculptor George Minne, while the *Second School of Latem* included Expressionists such as Constant Permeke. Today, their work is exhibited in major Belgian and international museums. The memory of the artists is kept alive in the *Museum Dhondt-Dhaenens (Tue–Sun 10am–5pm | admission 6 euros | Museumlaan 14 | tel. 09 2 82 51 23 | www.museumdd.be).*

Fine architecture in the Flemish late Gothic style: Oudenaarde town hall

Pomme d'Or (11 rooms | Markt 62 | tel. 055 3119 00 | www.pommedor.be | Moderate). Information: Dienst Toerisme | Markt 1 | tel. 055 3172 51 | www.oudenaarde.be

SINT-MARTENS-LATEM
(125 E4) *(ௐ F5)*

Sint-Martens-Latem (pop. 8200) used to be an artists' colony along the bendy, tranquilly picturesque Leie river, 5 km/3 miles southwest of Ghent. Members of the *First School of Latem* were the Impressionist painter Emile Claus and the

VLAAMSE ARDENNEN
(125 E–F5) *(ௐ F–G 7–8)*

The hilly country with its many waterways, mills, breweries and charming villages is ideal for relaxation. Towards the south, it segues into the *Pays des collines*, with *Ellezelles*, birthplace of Agatha Christie's detective Hercule Poirot *(Maison du Parc naturel du Pays des collines | Ruelle des Ecoles 1 | Ellezelles | tel. 068 54 46 00 | www.pays-des-collines.be).* Information: Dienst Toerisme Oudenaarde | Markt 1 | tel. 055 3172 51 | www.toerisme vlaamseardennen.be

FLEMISH BRABANT

Flemish Brabant is dominated by soft hills, lovely valleys, villages and little towns full of art. In the easterly Hageland, seamlessly merging into Limburg's Haspengouw, grapes thrive, yielding wine that will surprise you.

Most farmers here, however, earn their living growing sugar beet. Western Pajottenland, next to the rural part of the province of East Flanders, is where Gueuze beer is brewed. Right in the heart of this tranquil province, the scene in its capital Leuven has been dominated for centuries by students at Belgium's oldest university. To the west of the town, modern dormitories segue into the urban agglomeration around Brussels – where an entire new world awaits you.

BRUSSELS

(129 E–F2) (⊕ K–L 6–7) Belgium's capital city (Bruxelles, pop. 1.2 million), a city state within the federal kingdom, provides strong contrasts.

While there are two official languages, French and Flemish, the streets of Brussels resound to a Babylonian babble, as two fifths of the city's inhabitants are immigrants – rich ones from EU and NATO countries, poor ones from Morocco, Turkey or Central Africa. The city itself is full of contrasts and diversity, with soulless modern architecture alongside splendid historic buildings, and chic neighbourhoods bordering derelict ones. The popular lower town is much different

Photo: Palais du Roi in Brussels

A crescent around Belgium's capital city: varied farming country and the oldest university

🏙 WHERE TO START?
Grand' Place: the ideal starting point. Only a few minutes' walk and you'll be in the elegant Galeries Saint-Hubert shopping arcades or in the fashion quarter around Rue Dansaert, the cathedral, the major museums and the Palais du Roi. Multi-storey car parks in the immediate vicinity include Agora, Albertine, Monnaie. Metro 3, 4: Bourse; Metro 1, 5: Gare Centrale.

from the elegant upper town. The cultural attractions are beautiful Art Nouveau buildings, fabulous museums and the famous opera house, alongside the cultural centres Flagey and Palais des Beaux-Arts, both masterpieces of Art Deco. A cool alternative scene is experimenting in crossover projects in old factories. Brussels however doesn't boast about all it has; rather it invites you to go off and make your own discoveries.

For more in-depth information, consult the MARCO POLO guide to 'Brussels'.

ATOMIUM ★

Thanks to its stainless steel cladding and avant-garde light design by Ingo Maurer, the Atomium is now shining even brighter than it did at the 1958 World Exhibition. Inside the spheres you'll find exhibitions on the Fifties and contemporary art.

in this church: baptisms, weddings and funerals. *Parvis de Sainte-Gudule | Metro: Gare Centrale*

CENTRE BELGE DE LA BANDE DESSINÉE

The Belgians take comics, their 'ninth art' very seriously. The comic museum is housed in a bright warehouse by the pio-

A cosmopolitan air and splendid façades: terrace café on Grand´ Place

☆ Fabulous panoramic view across Brussels and surroundings from the (prohibitively expensive) restaurant in the uppermost sphere. *Daily 10am–6pm | admission 9 euros | Bd. Du Centenaire | www.atomium.be | Metro 1A: Heysel*

CATHÉDRALE SAINT-MICHEL ★

Dedicated to Saint Gundula and Saint Michael, the cathedral is the finest example of Brabant Gothic. Buried in the national church are the dukes of Brabant and Habsburg provincial governors. Since 1830, the Belgian royal family has held its festivities and commemorations

neer of Art Nouveau, Victor Horta. The museum presents the classics – Hergé, Edgar Jacobs and Peyo – alongside the national and international avant-garde. There's a nice brasserie here too. *Tue–Sun 10am–6pm | admission 7.50 euros | Rue des Sables 20 | Metro: Gare Centrale, De Brouckère*

GRAND' PLACE ★

One of the world's most beautiful squares, lined by splendid Baroque guild houses, is dominated by the late Gothic *City Hall (Hôtel de Ville | Tue/Wed 2.30–4pm, Sun 10am–12 noon | admission 3 euros),* which is sublime inside and out. There is a daily flower market too. *Metro: Bourse*

MUSÉES ROYAUX DES BEAUX-ARTS DE BELGIQUE ★ ●

Belgium's royal art museums shine with masterpieces of early Netherlands painting (Hieronymus Bosch, Hans Memling, Joachim Patinir, Rogier van der Weyden), and works by Pieter Bruegel the Elder (amongst them the 'Census at Bethlehem'), Peter Paul Rubens and Anthony van Dyck. The fin-de-siècle section shows top paintings by the Symbolists James Ensor and Fernand Khnopff, as well as divine Art Nouveau furniture and objects. Also worth seeing: the paintings of the Dutch and French school. *Tue–Sun 10am–5pm | admission 8 euros (combination ticket with Magritte Museum 13 euros) | Rue de la Régence 3 | www.fine-arts-museum.be | Metro: Gare Centrale*

MUSÉE MAGRITTE MUSEUM

The largest and best collection of works by the prominent Surrealist are housed in an enchanting shrine. Letters, photographs, films and objects provide deep insights into the artist's life, work and times. Tip: book tickets online! *Tue–Sun 10am–5pm | admission 8 euros | Place Royale 1 | www.musee-magritte-museum.be | Metro: Gare Centrale*

PALAIS DU ROI ●

In the neo-Baroque city palace, Belgians kings work and give state receptions, while Queen Paola fits the splendid edifice with works by contemporary Belgian artists. Do visit if you're around in the summer, if only for INSIDERTIP Jan Fabre's ceiling in the Hall of Mirrors, a glittering dream made from millions of beetle carapaces. *Late July–early Sept daily 9.30am–4pm | free admission | Place des Palais | Metro: Trône*

FOOD & DRINK

CAFÉ BELGA

Brussels' artists and creative folk, students of the Free University and young expats enjoy refreshing drinks and conversation to match in the former Broadcasting House. Huge terrace with romantic views of the ponds opposite. Nice breakfasts, international newspapers. *Sun–Thu 8am–2am, Fri/Sat 8am–3am | Place Eugène Flagey 1 | www.cafebelga.be | bus no. 71*

INSIDERTIP KWINT ● ☼

The long copper sculpture by star designer Arne Quinze below the ceiling vaults is as spectacular as the view of

---

MARCO POLO HIGHLIGHTS

★ **Atomium**
Day or night, this modern icon glows across all of Brussels → p. 60

★ **Cathédrale Saint-Michel**
In Brussels: a splendid backdrop for Belgian history → p. 60

★ **Grand' Place**
'The world's most beautiful theatre', Brussels' meeting place → p. 60

★ **Musées Royaux des Beaux-Arts de Belgique**
The nation's treasure chest – in Brussels → p. 61

★ **Stadhuis**
The gem of Brabant Gothic in Leuven → p. 65

★ **Diest**
Splendour in the provinces – and the small town is ideal for strolling → p. 66

Brussels and the imaginative dishes using caviar and truffles. Hip cocktail bar and terrace. Cosmopolitan clientele. *Closed Sun | Mont des Arts 1 | tel. 02 5 05 95 95 | www.kwintbrussels.com | Metro: Gare Centrale | Moderate*

IN 'T SPINNEKOPKE

In this cosy house dating back to 1762 they serve Brussels specialities, mainly prepared with beer – and that applies to fish and desserts too. Over 100 beers are served. Pleasant terrace. The clientele: Old Brussels, trend setters from the fashion quarter and expats. *Closed Sat lunchtime and Sun | Place du Jardin-aux-fleurs 1 | tel. 02 5 11 86 95 | www.spinnekopke. be | Métro Anneessens | Budget*

SHOPPING

Along the *Boulevard de Waterloo*, *Avenue de la Toison d'Or* and *Avenue -Louise* in the upper town, you'll find the luxury boutiques of the international designers, unusual boutiques in *Rue du Bailli* and *Rue du Page* as well as around the *Place du Châtelain, Place Brugmann* and *Place Saint-Boniface*. The stars of the Antwerp and Brussels scene (Jean-Paul Knott and Martin Margiela amongst them) cluster around *Rue Dansaert* in the lower town.

The alternative brands favour *Rue du Lombard,* the more traditional ones *Rue Neuve* with its major chain stores. Fancy traditional establishments (Delvaux, Neuhaus, Val Saint-Lambert) can be found in the elegant shopping arcades Galeries Saint-Hubert. The *Place du Jeu de Balle* has a *flea market (daily 6am–2pm),* the *Place du Grand Sablon* an *antiques market (Sat 9am–6pm, Sun 9am–2pm).* Distinguished antique dealers and art galleries reside in the side streets off Sablon.

The biggest and most colourful grocery market takes place around southern railway station *(Gare du Midi | Sun 6am–1pm).*

ENTERTAINMENT

Opera, *Flagey* (the arts centre located in the former broadcasting house), *Palais des Beaux-Arts,* some 50 theatres, various dance ensembles, jazz bands, pop and rock bands, one of the world's best cinematheques, avant-garde cinemas, hot clubs and trendy lounge bars, chic clubs, cosy hostelries – at night, Brussels is even more alive than in the daytime. Hotspots are the neighbourhoods around the university (students' pubs), around *Place Flagey* and *Place du Châtelain* (trendy Brussels folks and expats), *Place du Luxembourg* (young expats), *Rue Ar-*

LAMBIC, GUEUZE AND KRIEK

Lambic is the beer made with natural yeast and bacteria that waft through the air of Brussels and the Pajottenland to the west. On cool November days, the brewers boil up 65 per cent malt, 35 per cent wheat and three-year old hops. The mixture is filled into flat basins, triggering spontaneous fermentation. After

that the brew is left to mature for at least a year in wooden barrels. Various vintages of this *lambic* are blended, bottled and fermented like champagne. The slightly sour thirst-quenching result is called *gueuze*. For *kriek* cherry juice is added – the fruit for this traditionally being harvested in the Pajottenland.

chimède and side streets (older expats), as well as *Place Saint-Job* (yuppies). In the Lower Town, *Place Saint-Géry, Rue Dansaert* and *Rue de Flandre* attract all the trend setters, while gay life revolves around *Marché-au-Charbon*. Things are quieter around *Grand' Place* and *Sablon*. For an overview, consult the Wednesday supplement ('MAD') of 'Le Soir' daily newspaper and *www.agenda.be*.

WHERE TO STAY

BEMANOS
Luxurious boutique hotel between southern train station and city centre. Fab bathrooms styled in original designs, enchanting lounge with sun terrace, fine spa. *60 rooms | Square de l'Aviation 23–27 | tel. 02 5 20 65 65 | www.bemanos. com | Metro: Gare du Midi | Expensive*

HÔTEL PACIFIC
Intimate design hotel in the heart of the fashion quarter. Fabulously styled rooms and a welcoming Art Deco bar. *13 rooms | Rue Antoine Dansaert 57 | tel. 02 213 00 80 | www.hotelcafepacific.com | Metro: Bourse | Expensive*

INSIDER TIP THE WHITE HOTEL
Located in the trendy part of the Upper Town, this hotel boasts very spacious white rooms with cool designer furniture, some with terrace and panoramic views. Computer niches, guest scooters, organic breakfast, plus a lovely lounge. *53 rooms | Avenue Louise 212 | tel. 02 6 44 29 29 | www.thewhitehotel.be | tram 94: Bailli | Moderate*

INFORMATION

Visit Brussels | Rue Royale 2–4 and city hall (Grand' Place) | tel. 02 5 13 89 40 | www.visitbrussels.be

WHERE TO GO

JARDIN BOTANIQUE NATIONAL
(129 E2) (*ω K6*)
Just under 3 km/2 miles north of the Atomium lie Belgium's National Botanic Gardens. In the moated castle of

Brussels offers plenty of options to enjoy opera and theatre

Bouchout inside landscaped gardens covering nearly 100 ha, Empress Charlotte of Mexico once passed her long declining years. Plant lovers can explore many corners filled with hydrangeas, magnolias, rhododendrons and decorative shrubs. The main attraction is the ● *Palais des Plantes,* a miniature town consisting of 30 glass greenhouses, of which 13 are open to the public. 18,000 species of plants are cultivated here, specialising in the various vegetation zones of Central Africa. The presentation of 500 million years of evolution is fascinating. The shop sells fun souvenirs such as seeds, two kinds of honey and chicory jam. *April–Sept daily 9.30am–6.30pm, Oct–March daily 9.30am–5pm | admission 5 euros | Domaine de Bouchout | Nieuwelaan 38 | Meise | www.jardinbotanique.be | buses De Lijn 250, 251 from Atomium or Gare du Nord*

LEUVEN

(130 A5) (*ꜛ M6*) Leuven (Louvain, pop. 87,000) is the main university town in Flanders. Over 25,000 students studying at the Catholic University, founded in 1425, and thousands of young college students ensure high spirits.
During the university breaks, rock, folk and other festivals put some swing into the town. Leuven however can also look back on a proud history. This is where the dukes of Leuven built up their duchy of Brabant in the 10th century. While Leuven suffered badly in both World Wars, it still maintains many picturesque corners perfect for a quiet stroll.

SIGHTSEEING

CENTRALE UNIVERSITEITS-BIBLIOTHEEK
Following World War I, American sponsors donated the imposing central library with carillon in the tower. The old library had been burned down in 1914 by the Germans. *Monseigneur Ladeuzeplein*

GROOT BEGIJNHOF
The Great Beguinage is a small town within the town, restored in the 1960s by the university. The well-kept houses accommodate visiting professors, doctoral students and bursary-holders. The Gothic church has a magnificent Baroque interior. The most romantic spots of the Beguinage can be found along the Dijle stream. *Schapenstraat*

M MUSEUM
This splendid old palace gives visitors an idea of how Leuven's patrician families once lived. The impressive new building by Stéphane Beel is devoted to masterful late Gothic wooden sculptures, excellent changing exhibitions and the ☼ INSIDER TIP roof terrace with panoramic views. *Tue–Sun 11am–6pm | admission 9 euros (combination ticket, also granting admission to the treasury*

of the Sint-Pieterskerk) | Vanderkelen-straat 28 | www.mleuven.be

SINT-PIETERSKERK

The most impressive feature of the Gothic main church is the interior with its clear lines. The exterior is more modest, partly because the church was never given a tower. A Gothic triforium with a spectacular, tall triumphal cross divides off the choir. The pulpit is a masterpiece of baroque wood carving. The choir and its lateral chapels shelter precious works of art, amongst them the 'Last Supper' (1464–68) by outstanding Leuven painter Dieric Bouts. *Tue–Sat (15 March–15 Oct Mon too) 10am–5pm, Sun 2–5pm | admission 2.50 euros (9 euros for combination ticket with M Museum)*

STADHUIS ★

Leuven's town hall is a treasure chest in stone. This super-ornate edifice designed by famous architect Jan Keldermans and others counts among the highlights of late Brabant Gothic style, even if the sculptures of Leuven dignitaries and many other details were only added in the period between 1841 and 1892. *Grote Markt 9*

FOOD & DRINK

WERELDCAFÉ.COOP ⏱

Students and intellectuals, green politicians and socially active clerics meet in this café-cum-brasserie. INSIDER TIP Only organic and fair trade products. *Variable opening times | Helleputteplein 4 | tel. mobile 0474 41 08 22 | www.wereldcafe.be | Budget*

DE WIERING

Brasserie in a super-cosy house, spread across several floors, roof terrace. Good solid fare, including vegetarian options. *Daily | Wieringstraat 2 | tel. 016 29 15 45 | www.dewiering.be | Budget*

ZARZA

Modern, warm design, pretty veranda and a lively bar. Tasty beery dishes, good

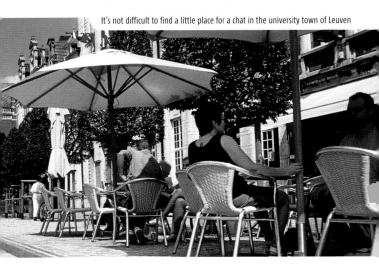

It's not difficult to find a little place for a chat in the university town of Leuven

selection of salads, kids' fare too. *Closed Sun | Bondgenotenlaan 92 | tel. 016 20 50 05 | www.zarza.be | Moderate*

ENTERTAINMENT

Being a student town means there are hundreds of places for revelry – and no formal curfew. *Grote Markt*, *Oude Markt*, *Muntstraat* and *Tiensestraat* in the centre form the heart of the action.

DE BLAUWE SCHUIT
Retro-style pub with a pretty garden. *Daily | Vismarkt 16*

CHESS CAFÉ
Hip meeting point where you can play chess too. Live jazz and blues concerts on Thu evenings; on Sat and Sun DJs animate some dancing action. Wok dishes available. *Sun–Thu 12 noon–3pm and 6pm–midnight, Fri/Sat 6pm–2am | Fonteinstraat 1A*

LOW BUDGET

▶ At weekends and during holidays, hotels in Brussels offer substantial discounts: check out *www.visit brussels.be*.

▶ *Arsène50* sells tickets to over 100 events venues at half price for performances on the same day. *Tue–Sat 12.30–5.30pm | Rue Royale 2–4 | Brussels | www.arsene50.be*

▶ Keep an eye open for the regular free jazz, folk and pop concerts happening on Brussels Grand' Place. *www.visitbrussels.be*

DOMUS
A maze of rooms across several floors, with a terrace and great vibes, fuelled by beer on tap from the in-house brewery. Simple dishes help soak up the excess. *Daily | Tiensestraat 8*

WHERE TO STAY

MARTIN'S KLOOSTER
This fine quiet hotel was created inside the palace of Emperor Charles V, which went on to be used as a monastery. Salon with fireplace, elegant courtyard, extensive gardens, spacious rooms, car park. *103 rooms | Predikherenstaat 22 | tel. 016 213141 | www.kloosterhotel.com | Expensive*

GASTHOF DE PASTORIJ
Friendly hotel suitable for families, central location yet quiet. Comfortable rooms, generous breakfast. *7 rooms | Sint-Michielsstraat 5 | tel. 016 82 21 09 | www.depastorij.be | Moderate*

INFORMATION

Dienst Toerisme | Naamsestraat 3 | tel. 016 20 30 20 | www.leuven.be

WHERE TO GO

DIEST ★ (130 B4) *(⑰ O5–6)*
This small town (pop. 22,000) occupies a picturesque location between a bend in the Demer stream and a green hill topped by a citadel, 27 km/17 miles northeast of Leuven. The *Grote Markt* is dominated by the *Sint-Sulpitiuskerk.* The Gothic western part of the edifice consists of French limestone, the nave and choir of the local reddish-brown iron sandstone. The interior is dominated by a late Gothic triumphal cross, the Baroque high altar and the Baroque pulpit. Philip William of

Oranje-Nassau is buried in the choir. The ducal dynasty were the de facto owners of Diest between 1499 and 1794. In the cloisters the *treasury (July/Aug Tue–Sun 2–5pm, May/June and Sept Sat–Sun 2–5pm | admission 1.50 euros)* has a display of precious gems. Also on the market square, the *town hall* is an elegant neoclassical construction. In the cellar vaults,

ZOUTLEEUW (130 B5) (*∅ O7*)

37 km/23 miles east of Leuven, this sleepy small town (pop. 7700) is surrounded by the little river Gete and the well-watered nature reserve *De Vinne*. The Gothic *Sint-Leonarduskerk (April–Sept Tue–Sun 10am–12 noon and 1.30–5pm, Oct–March Tue–Fri 10am–12 noon and 1.30–4pm | admission 2 euros)* is filled to

Little town with plenty of atmosphere: on Diest's Grote Markt

the *Stadsmuseum De Hofstadt (May–Sept daily 10am–12 noon and 1–5pm, closed Oct–April Mon and public holidays | admission 4 euros)* present all aspects of the history and crafts of Diest. A Baroque gate leads into the *Begijnhof* where 90 individual and community houses form a small town within the town, of crooked cobbled lanes. Many more monuments, *Warande Park* in the town centre and the green surroundings are an invitation to keep walking. *Information: Toerisme Diest | Grote Markt 1 | tel. 013 35 32 74 | www.toerismediest.be*

overflowing with precious works of art. On the other side of the market square you'll find the *Renaissance town hall, with the medieval cloth hall* – which explains for the wealth of the little town. Today, it houses the friendly *Lakenhal tavern (closed Mon)* with terrace. This is where they serve the fruity wines of the Hageland northwest of the town. The *Stedelijke Toeristische Dienst (Markt 11 | tel. 011 78 12 88 | www.zoutleeuw.be)* – also inside the cloth hall – INSIDERTIP has some of those rare wines for sale.

ANTWERP

Antwerp enjoys world-wide fame as a global port. The diamond trade too adds its ha-penny worth to the GDP of all Flanders, while the fashion business provides additional glamour.

The industry and trade of the city of Antwerp can sometimes displace the realisation that there is a province of Antwerp too – with beautiful natural surroundings outside the city, as well as historic towns such as Mechelen and Turnhout. Extending to the north of the Albert Canal, the Kempen landscape has poor sandy soils, pines, birches and heather, with scattered dreamy lakes and quiet canals, moors, tranquil villages and enchanting abbeys. To the south of the Albert Canal, fields and greenhouses dominate the landscape. The fertile soils

support potatoes and vegetables, fruit and flowers, sold on the wholesale market in Sint-Katelijne-Waver. The chicory and asparagus of the region are famous, and the high-quality *Mechelse Koekoek* chickens are a hot commodity amongst gourmets.

ANTWERP

MAP INSIDE BACK COVER
(127 D–E 4–5) (*ひ K–L 3–4*) *Sinjoren*, masters, is what the proud Antwerpians call themselves, and their city (pop. 470,000) is a *metropool* of course. In the capital Brussels, they claim, money is spent, in Antwerp it is earned.
All of Belgium laughs about this grand-

Photo: Grote Markt in Antwerp

The shining heart of Flanders: an attractive province surrounds the region's vibrant economic and cultural second city

🏙 WHERE TO START?

Grote Markt: the market square with the town hall is centrally located. A lane leads to the cathedral, and it's only a few minutes to the Rubenshuis, Plantin Moretus Museum, Fashion Museum, shopping areas and river Schelde. Car parks: Groenplaats, Meir, Rubens. From the train station trams no. 2, 15 (destination Linkeroever) to Groenplaats.

standing. Yet who can blame the *sinjoren* for viewing their city as the navel of Belgium?

Antwerp's port happens to be the second-largest in Europe. Four specialised exchanges trade over half all the world's diamonds – both raw and cut. Antwerp is a hothouse for fashion designers, painters and musicians, attracting theatre directors, dancers, poets and publishers – the cultural scene ensures a lively buzz. And the whole thing is embedded in a historical perspective: in the 16th

Antwerp – a vibrant city, yet also a place to stroll at leisure

century, the town on the Schelde river was amongst Europe's leading hubs of trade and finance. Following the commotion of the Wars of Religion, the Counter-reformation triggered another golden age, when Peter Paul Rubens and Anthony van Dyck lit up the world of art. Despite heavy German bombardments in the winter of 1944/45, many buildings and art treasures still testify to the glorious past of a city with a vibrancy encountered nowhere else in Flanders.

SIGHTSEEING

CENTRAAL STATION
The central station, built in the neo-Renaissance style, is a sublime monument to the industrial age. The marble station hall and imposing staircase would not look out of place in a palace. *Koningin Astridplein*

CONSCIENCEPLEIN
Peter Paul Rubens designed the elegant Baroque façade, the high altar and the Lady Chapel of the *Sint-Carolus-Borromaeus Jesuit church.* Next door the priests built their seminary. The popular square with a monument to writer Hendrik Conscience is given a graceful touch by a softly bubbling fountain.

DIAMANTMUSEUM
Behind an Art Deco façade, the Diamond Museum provides an introduction to the world of *steentje*, as Antwerpians call the glittering stones. Photographs document the extraction process, the geological background and technical applications are explained, and a polisher demonstrates his skills live. Most fascinating of all are the precious jewels, of which plenty are on view here, including copies of the British crown jewels. *Thu–Tue 10am–5.30pm, closed Jan | admission 6 euros | Koningin Astridplein 19–23 | www.diamantmuseum.be*

DIAMANTWIJK
The quarter housing the diamond trade forms an 'S' between *Rijpstraat, Hove-*

niersstraat and *Schupstraat.* Stressed dealers hurry through this mini-Manhattan: orthodox Jews, Indians, Lebanese, Russians. Masses of security cameras, bodyguards and police eyeball every passer-by. After all, some 45 billion euros changes hands here every year.

INSIDER TIP 'T EILANDJE

The old port is now the hip quarter in the north of the city, inviting visitors to explore at leisure. Warehouses have been converted into lofts, theatres and clubs. Star architects Hans Kollhoff and Richard Meier created spectacular new buildings. Yachts bob up and down by the quayside. At the *Rijnkaai*, the American architects' office of Beyer, Blinder, Belle is converting the former terminal of the Red Star Line into a *Museum of Emigration and Immigration*. Glamour aside, the ambience is rougher than in the Zuid quarter.

PHOTO MUSEUM

Impressive and dynamically run venue showing current trends alongside the classics – and even good snap-shots by complete amateurs. *Tue–Sun 10am–5pm | admission 6 euros | Waalse Kaai 47 | www.fotomuseum.be*

GROTE MARKT

Antwerp's market square with the *town hall* forms an enlarged triangle. The sturdy Renaissance building was designed by Cornelis Floris in 1561, with the monumental *Brabo Fountain* in front dating to 1887. Most houses on this square were built around 1900 as inns.

HARBOUR TRIPS

Covering 13,500 ha, Europe's second port is simply huge, with additional docks planned for the left bank of the river Schelde. There is bustling movement here by day and night. The two-hour harbour tour is an experience in itself, but a INSIDER TIP *Candlelight Cruise* is particularly impressive. *Port tour May–Sept daily 1.30pm, Oct–Nov Fri–Sun 10.30am and 1.30pm (14.50 euros) | Candlelight Cruise 1st and 3rd Sat of the month, 7.30pm (69*

MARCO POLO HIGHLIGHTS

⭐ MAS
The museum by the river offers the most fabulous panoramic views – and it's free → p. 72

⭐ ModeNatie
In Antwerp: temple of the young Flemish fashion scene → p. 73

⭐ Onze-Lieve-Vrouwekathedraal
Magnificent Gothic architecture in Antwerp, full of Rubens paintings → p. 73

⭐ Plantin-Moretus-Museum
In the humanists' printing works in Antwerp, time has stood still → p. 74

⭐ Rubenshuis
At home with the master in studio, residence and garden: Peter Paul Rubens had the city palace in Antwerp built for himself in 1610 → p. 74

⭐ Sint-Romboutskathedraal
Imposing seat of the cardinal archbishop in Mechelen with two carillons that are played regularly → p. 82

⭐ Abdij van Averbode
Right amongst forests and meadows, discover the most beautiful abbey in Flanders, with its magnificent Baroque church → p. 83

euros) | departure Londenbrug/Havenkaai 14 | www.flandria.nu

KONINKLIJK MUSEUM VOOR SCHONE KUNSTEN

At the centre of attention in this magnificent neoclassical building are monumental works by world-famous Baroque

the MAS (Museum aan de Stroom) in the old port is 60 m/196 ft high. The ● ⛵ boulevard of escalators leads up to the viewing platform on the 10th floor for ravishing panoramic views of the city and surroundings. Rooms without daylight illustrate Antwerp's history, the development of shipping, everyday life and cus-

Open-air art: the Middelheimmuseum's landscaped park

painters: Peter Paul Rubens, Anthony van Dyck and Jacob Jordaens. They are joined by masterpieces of both old Netherlandish painting (Hans Memling, Jan van Eyck) and Belgian Modernism (James Ensor, Rik Wouters). *Closed for renovation until approx. 2017 | Leopold de Waelplaats | www.kmska.be*

MAS ★

The tower of sandstone and undulating glass that architects Willem Jan Neutelings and Miechiel Riedijck designed for

toms in this multicultural city. On the 8th floor is an exquisite INSIDER TIP collection of precious pre-Columbian artefacts. The square in front of the museum is adorned with the huge 'Dead Skull' mosaic by Luc Tuymans. The museum also has a cafeteria with a fine terrace and an excellent shop. *Boulevard daily 9.30am–midnight, free admission | museum Tue–Sun 10am–5pm, admission 5 euros (combined ticket museum/special exhibitions 10 euros), last Wed of the month free admission | Hanzestedenplaats 1 | www.mas.be*

MIDDELHEIMMUSEUM ●

This 30-ha landscaped park holds hundreds of monumental sculptures by Jean Arp, Henry Moore and Auguste Rodin. The collection is extended every year. Two modern pavilions designed by Renaat Braem and Paul Robbrecht show more fragile sculptures and changing exhibitions, while the little neo-Baroque palace harbours the visitor centre, cafeteria and shop. *Tue–Sun Oct–March 10am–5pm, April and Sept 10am–7pm, May and Aug 10am–8pm, June/July 10am–9pm | admission free | Middelheimlaan 61 | www.middelheimmuseum.be*

MODENATIE ★

The fascinating construction by architect Marie-José van Hee houses the *MoMu* fashion museum with attractive exhibitions, the fashion department of the art college and display cases for avant-garde projects as well as the *Flanders' Fashion Institute,* which promotes the work of the city's designers all over the world. The fantastic library is open to the public free of charge, and the bookshop INSIDER TIP *Copyright (www.copyrightbookshop.be)* has an excellent selection. *Tue–Sun 10am–6pm | admission 8 euros | Nationalestraat 28 | www.momu.be*

MUSEUM VOOR HEDENDAAGSE KUNST (MUHKA)

A huge grain warehouse on the old port has been converted into a museum of contemporary art. The collection is always presented afresh, and changing exhibitions and workshops for children are held too. The roof now has a new café with a mural by Keith Haring as well as two large ☀️ terraces with fabulous views. *Tue–Sun 10am–6pm | admission 8 euros | Leuvensestraat 32 | www.muhka.be*

MUSEUM MAYER VAN DEN BERGH

Following the death of collector Fritz Mayer van den Bergh in 1901, his mother had this museum built in the style of an old patrician residence. On view are precious old Netherlandish painting, furniture, sculptures and tapestries. Amongst the highlights are a lavishly painted breviary and Pieter Bruegel's 'Dulle Griet'. *Tue–Sun 10am–5pm | admission 8 euros, combination ticket with Rubenshuis 10 euros | Lange Gasthuisstraat 19 | www.museummayervandenbergh.be*

MUSEUM VLEESHUIS

This splendid Gothic meat market is 500 years old. Instruments, paintings, engravings alongside modern audiovisual media illustrate all aspects of 600 years of music and dance in the city. *Tue–Sun 10am–5pm | admission 5 euros | Vleeshouwersstraat 38–40 | www.museumvleeshuis.be*

ONZE-LIEVE-VROUWEKATHEDRAAL ★

The exterior of the Gothic Cathedral of Our Lady with its unfinished tower seems fragmented. Inside, a bright taller transept and the choir adjoin the broad nave with double aisles. This is where you'll find famous Rubens paintings: in the transept the 'Raising of the Cross' (1610) and the 'Deposition from the Cross' (1624), and, in the centre of the Baroque high altar, the 'Assumption of the Virgin Mary' (1626; the lady clad in red by the grave represents Rubens' first wife Isabella Brant, who died in 1626 of the plague) and the 'Resurrection of Christ' (1612) in the second chapel on the right. Regular organ concerts, carillon concerts on Monday evenings. The ☀️ tower offers wonderful views. *Mon–Fri 10am–5pm, Sat 10am–3pm, Sun 1–4pm | admission 5 euros | Handschoenmarkt | www.dekathedraal.be*

PLANTIN MORETUS MUSEUM ⭐

In 1548 the French printer Christophe Plantin settled in Antwerp. After Plantin's death, his son-in-law Jan Moretus took over the *Officina Plantiniana,* which published important humanist manuscripts, as well as Bible translations, dictionaries and musical scores. In 1876, Edward Moretus sold the Renaissance-era estate with the entire furnishings to the city. Here you can admire precious furniture in den ornate salons on the ground floor, with Rubens portraits hanging on the walls. The first floor holds two imposing libraries. The workshops, offices and storerooms too are reminders of this printing dynasty. *Tue–Sun 10am–5pm | admission 8 euros | Vrijdagmarkt 22 | museum.antwerpen.be/plantin_moretus*

ROCKOXHUIS

Time seems to have stood still in the patrician palace and former residence of the humanist mayor Nicolaas Rockox (1560–1640). Precious furniture and tapestries, as well as some of the oldest Flemish landscape paintings in existence, lend splendour to the house. *Tue–Sun 10am–5pm | admission 2.50 euros | Keizerstraat 12 | museum.antwerpen.be/rockoxhuis*

RUBENSHUIS ⭐

Not only did Peter Paul Rubens paint Europe's elite, he was also a passionate collector and skilled diplomat. The Renaissance palace which he built for himself in 1610 – including a pantheon for his precious objects, studio and pleasure garden – reflects his status. Amongst the highlights are some of the master's most beautiful (self) portraits. Regular exhibitions of international calibre are held here as well. *Tue–Sun 10am–5pm | admission 8 euros, combined ticket with Museum Mayer van den Bergh 10 euros | Wapper 9–11 | www.rubenshuis.be*

SINT-ANNATUNNEL

Between 1931 and 1933 a tunnel was constructed under the Schelde in order to connect the historic centre with the new residential quarters on the left bank. Old-fashioned escalators and elevators in white-tiled Art Deco staircases take pedestrians down. From 〽 *Linkeroever* you'll enjoy fabulous views of Old Antwerp. *Sint-Jansvliet*

SINT-JACOBSKERK

The sturdy Gothic tower and the massive transept of this church dominate the Old Town. Inside, the Baroque splendour of black and white marble, silver and brass

ANTWERP PERSONAL SHOPPER

The sheer number of boutiques by Belgian and international fashion designers, plus the shops selling vintage and second-hand clothing, are a bit confusing for some fashionistas: which style are they looking for, where should they head for first, how do you say 'no, thanks' in style if you don't like something? The solution: *personal shoppers*. They gather preliminary information on interests and requests, prepare boutique visits and accompany the shopping expedition. They don't just chat about fashion, but many other aspects of the city too. *www.dn-travel.be | www.recycleyourwardrobe.be | www.tanguyottomer.com*

awaits. Here Peter Paul Rubens married his second wife, Hélène Fourment, in 1630, and the five children of this marriage were christened. Reigning supreme in his time, the painter was laid to rest in the chapel behind the high altar. The Virgin Mary on the altarpiece bears a strong facial resemblance to Hélène Fourment. *April–Oct daily 2–5pm | admission 2 euros | Lange Nieuwstraat 73–75 | www.topa.be*

STEEN

The oldest building in Antwerp – erected between 1200 and 1225 – was originally a mighty fortress defending the town and port. In the 19th century then the biggest part of the complex was torn down in order to straighten the quay walls. Today's port promenade is popular with tourists and locals out for a stroll. *Steenplein 1*

Rubenshuis in Antwerp: the famous painter's residence, studio and garden

SINT-PAULUSKERK

On the outside, the church presents an elegant late Gothic style. The Baroque interior is a true treasure chest: the best wood carvers made the choir chairs and confessionals, and the most famous painters in the city (Anthony van Dyck amongst them) designed the 15 Mysteries of the Rosary. The magnificent image of the Virgin Mary is a masterful Caravaggio copy. The fine Baroque organ is regularly used for concerts. *May–Sept daily 2–5pm | free admission | Veemarkt 14 | www.topa.be*

ZUID

In the 1990s, the filled-in basin of the old port became *the place to be.* Warehouses and trading offices were turned into modern museums and theatres, art galleries and designer shops, cool bars and restaurants, chic offices and lofts. This quarter boasts a fair number of spectacular new buildings by big-name architects, the highlight being the law courts by Richard Rogers, Ove Arup and Partners with its striking copper roofs. *Vlaamse Kaai/Waalse Kaai*

ZURENBORG

In the late 19th century, entrepreneurs Cogels and Osy built the most modern quarter of the city at the time. The roughly 200 façades are neo-Gothic, neo-Baroque, imitation Renaissance or sub-Art Nouveau from Brussels. Today still, these

CAFÉ-RESTAURANT DE KAAI ☼

Hangar in the old port, terrace with gorgeous views of the Schelde river. At the weekend dancing from about 11pm. Open to 2am. *Closed Sat lunchtime and Sun | Rijnkaai 94 | tel. 03 2 33 25 07 | www. de-kaai.be | Moderate*

Post-sightseeing: relaxed leisure time in one of Antwerp's many cafés

remnants of Antwerp's Belle Époque continue to be super trendy. *Cogels-Osylei | Berchem railway station*

FOOD & DRINK

INSIDER TIP AAHAAR

Friendly Indian restaurant putting on a varied vegetarian buffet for 9 euros! *Daily | Lange Herentalsestraat 23 | tel. 03 2 26 00 52 | www.aahaar.com | Budget*

BIJ LAM & YIN

This restaurant serves light fresh Chinese cuisine with the odd Belgian touch. *Closed Mon/Tue and at lunchtime | Reyndersstraat 17 | tel. 03 2 32 88 38 | Moderate*

DÔME-SUR-MER

Fresh shellfish and good fish dishes sold from a large counter. Laid-back atmosphere, fashionable clientele. *Closed Sat lunchtime and Sun/Mon | Arendstraat 1 | tel. 03 2 81 74 33 | www.domeweb.be | Moderate*

INSIDER TIP THE GLORIOUS

Wine bar with oriental décor in the trendy Zuid neighbourhood offering an excellent choice of wines by the glass and tasty bistro dishes. *Closed Mon | De Burburestraat 4a | tel. 03 2 37 06 13 | www.theglorious.be | Budget–Moderate*

HET GEBAAR LUNCH LOUNGE

In a cottage in the Botanical Gardens, Roger van Damme invents fabulous molecular dishes and patisserie. Reservations a must! Open 11am–6pm. *Closed Sun/Mon | Leopoldstraat 24 | tel. 03 2 93 72 32 | www.hetgebaar.be | Expensive*

LOMBARDIA

'Food for the people' is served in this slightly quirky rendezvous with terrace. Fresh vegetable and fruit juices, ginger tea, soups and tapas. Open 8am–6pm. *Closed Sun | Lombardenvest 78*

ZUIDERTERRAS ● ☼

Modern café-restaurant above the Schelde in the shape of a steamer. Fabulous views, open daily to midnight. *Ernest Van Dijckkaai 37 | tel. 03 2 34 12 75 | www. zuiderterras.be | Budget*

SHOPPING

Antwerp is paradise for shoppers. For chain stores look no further than the *Meir,* while luxury boutiques congregate around *Huidevettersstraat* and *Schuttershofstraat.* The boutiques of Antwerp's fashion designers and fabulous second-hand shops cluster around *Nationalestraat,* while trends beyond the mainstream are on offer in *Kammenstraat.* Trendy art galleries and interior design shops await in the *Zuid* quarter and on *Mechelse Steenweg,* fine antiques around *Conscienceplein* and *Leopoldstraat,* and second-hand items in *Kloosterstraat.* Expensive jewellers can be found between *Vestingstraat* and *Rijpstaat.*

The *Sunday market (8am–1pm)* on Oude Vaartplaats is gigantic. Remainders and goods from liquidation sales are auctioned off at *Vrijdagmarkt (Fri 9am–1pm).*

ANTWERPS KOOKHUYS

A dream for (amateur) chefs who will find everything they could possibly need here. *Terninckstraat 1 | www.antwerps kookhuys.be*

RECORD COLLECTOR

Huge selection of LPs and CDs old and new, with blues, jazz, pop and rock, many selling for only 1 euro. *Lange Koepoortstraat 70*

INSIDER TIP GÜNTHER WATTÉ

Unusual chocolate creations, finest tartlets and exclusive coffee brands; everything can be enjoyed in this elegant café in the fashion quarter. *Closed Mon | Steenhouwersvest 30*

DE WINKELHAAK

This new centre for young Flemish designers in a colourful lively neighbourhood is joined by several design stores in the neighbourhood. *Lange Winkelhaakstraat 26 | www.winkelhaak.be*

XSO

Super-modern stylish shop for fashion pieces ranging from Issey Miyake to Tim Van Steenbergen. *Eiermarkt 13–17 | www. xso.be*

SPORTS & ACTIVITIES

BADBOOT ☙

A barge converted into a swimming pool, with cool sun terraces, lounge bar and restaurant, situated in a wide harbour basin of the trendy 't Eilandje neighbourhood. In winter, the pool turns into an ice-skating rink, also used for curling. During and after sundown the ambience is sheer magic. Note that reservations are obligatory for the pool and ice rink! The *Badboot* also has strong eco credentials: the water used for swimming and showering is filtered in gravel bedding planted with dune grass. In cooler weather the water is placed in a storage tank below the basin to retain the heat as much as possible. Once night falls, the *Badboot* is lit by LED. *Daily 10am–10pm, lounge bar 10am–midnight | admission 4 euros per hour | Kattendijkdok Oostkaai 20 | www.badboot.be*

ENTERTAINMENT

There is also a throbbing clubbing scene in the former red-light district between *Orteliuskaai* and *Paardenmarkt*, with numerous bars between *De Keyserlei* and *Gemeentestraat*. The style brigade like the *Zuid* neighbourhood, while a more settled crowd enjoys the area around *Conscienceplein* and *Theaterplein,* and the old port of *'t Eilandje* is a strong new contender on the nightlife scene.

AMUZ ●
This unique music venue in the Baroque Augustine church exclusively puts on historical interpretations on original instruments, from medieval times to the 1930s, and also organises the *Laus polyphoniae festival. Kammenstraat 81 | tel. 03 2 02 46 69 | www.amuz.be*

INSIDERTIP CAFÉ KULMINATOR
Top beer pub, serving over 600 special brews. *Closed Sun | Vleminckveld 32*

DE MUZE
Leading jazz club, pleasantly intimate. Nearly every day live concerts after 10pm. *Daily noon–4am | Melkmarkt 15*

NOXX
The cathedral amongst the clubs has been styled to within an inch of its life by star designers. The big dance floor is flanked by smaller ones playing various sounds from house to lounge. VIP lounges, separate cubicles with VIP service, restaurant. The undisputed place to be right now. *Thu 11pm–6am, Fri/Sat 11pm–7am | Straatsburgdok/Noordkaai | www.noxxantwerp.be*

RED & BLUE
One of the biggest gay clubs in Europe is located in the new hipster neighbourhood. Young clientele, cosmopolitan ambience. In August, the club also organises the gay festival *Navigaytion (www.navigaytion.be). Fri/Sat 11pm–7am | Lange Schipperskapelstraat 11–13 | www.redandblue.be*

DE SINGEL
Hip arts centre for modern dance, avantgarde theatre and all musical genres. *Desguinlei 25 | tel. 03 2 48 28 28 | www.desingel.be*

WHERE TO STAY

Nice if occasionally a little pricey bed and breakfasts and holiday apartments can be found through *www.gastenkamers antwerpen.be*; furnished apartments (1–4 bedrooms) for longer stays are available from *www.antwerpflats.be.* General hotel bookings: *www.visitantwerpen.be.*

HOTEL BANKS
Design hotel in the heart of the fashion quarter, trendy café, lounge and roof terrace. *70 rooms | Steenhouwersvest 55 | tel. 03 2 32 40 02 | www.hotelbanks.be | Budget*

INSIDERTIP DOCKLANDS HOTEL
Modern, comfortable hotel in the new trendy neighbourhood. *32 rooms | Kempisch Dok Westkaai 84–90 | tel. 03 2 31 07 26 | www.docklandshotel.be | Moderate*

PULCINELLA

Cool, stylish, comfortable youth hostel right in the heart of the fashion quarter. The chic bar is worth a visit too. *47 rooms. (162 beds) | Bogaardeplein 1 | tel. 03 2 34 03 14 | www.jeugdherbergen.be | Budget*

DE WITTE LELIE

Elegant Baroque palace in the historical centre, with wonderful salons clustering around a patio, fabulous rooms and classy service. Underground car park. *10 rooms | Keizerstraat 16–18 | tel. 03 2 26 19 66 | www.dewittelelie.be | Expensive*

summer there are organ and carillon concerts. Travelling there by bike, through fields and forests along the Turnhout–Dessel canal, is a special experience (22 km/14 miles, bike hire from *Fietspunt* at Turnhout station). *Abdijlaan 16B | tel. 014 37 81 21 | www.abdijpostel.be*

ARBORETUM KALMTHOUT ☺
(127 E3) (*m L2*)

In 1857, a landscape designer started laying out these botanical gardens. 12 km/7.5 miles north of Antwerp, they cover 12 ha. All year round, visitors are

In the Arboretum Kalmthout, visitors can spend an educational day at any time of the year

INFORMATION

Antwerp Toerisme & Congres | Grote Markt 13 | tel. 03 2 32 01 03 | www.visitantwerpen.be

WHERE TO GO

ABDIJ VAN POSTEL (130 C2) (*m P3*)

45 km/28 miles east of Antwerp, amidst extensive forests, this Norbertine abbey with Romanesque church has a richly appointed library and a shop selling traditional products made by the monks. In

fascinated by thousands of plants, all exactly described. The hamamelis (witch hazel) and hellebores grown by Jelena De Belder enjoy world-wide fame. In January and February, INSIDER TIP hamamelis festivals are held. Excellent shop with plants, gardening tools and specialised literature, cafeteria. *15 March–15 Nov daily 10am–5pm, guided tours 11am and 2pm | admission 4 euros | Kalmthout | Heuvel 2 | www.arboretumkalmthout.be | Access via N1 and N117 or by train Antwerp–Essen (Kalmthout station)*

KALMTHOUTSE HEIDE
(127 E3) (*ᗈ K–L2*)

Only a few miles from the port, pure nature awaits: the heath landscape with its wonderful sand dunes and tranquil lakes covers 37.5 sq km/14.5 sq miles, including 57 km/ 35 miles of signposted hiking and biking trails. *Access via N11 and N122 or by train Antwerp–Essen (Heide station); information: Dienst Toerisme | Putsesteenweg 129 | Kalmthout | www.vvvkalmthout.be*

TURNHOUT (130 B2) (*ᗈ N3*)

Turnhout (pop. 38,500, 32 km/20 miles northeast of Antwerp) is a lively town clustering around the *moated castle* of the dukes of Brabant, an elegant brick edifice that acquired its current appearance in the 16th century. With its monumental Baroque high altar, confessionals and pulpit, as well as a superb Baroque organ (1662) and large carillon in the church tower (regular concerts), the *Sint-Pieterskerk* on the town hall square is a gem of late Brabantine Gothic. A mighty gate leads into the tranquil *beguinage (Begijnhof museum Tue–Sat 2–5pm, Sun 11am–5pm | admission 2.50 euros | Begijnhof 56)* with old linden trees and a fine Baroque church.

In the early 19th century, the paper industry emerged in Turnhout, specialising in playing cards. The splendid *Nationaal Museum van de Speelkaart (Tue–Sat 2–3pm, Sun 11am–5pm | admission 5 euros | Druivenstraat 18 | www.speelkaartenmuseum.be)* is dedicated to them. Machines show how the cards are produced. Every other year in December (2013, 2015 etc.) the *De Warande* arts centre puts on the biggest INSIDERTIP comics festival in Flanders *(www.stripturnhout.be)*.

In the town centre, the romantic *bed & breakfast Bon-Bon Jour/Nuit (3 rooms | Victoriestraat 10 | tel. mobile 0494 78 88 37 | www.bonbonjournuit.be | Mod-erate)* boasts an in-house confectionery, café, small spa and owners happy to provide information on their town. *Priorij Corsendonk (47 rooms plus 31 former monks' cells | Corsendonk 5 | Oud-Turnhout | tel. 014 46 28 00 | www.corsendonk.be | Moderate)* is a former monastery which gave its name to the stout beer of the same name. Good restaurant serving Belgian cuisine. *Information: Toerisme Turnhout | Grote Markt 14 | tel. 014 44 33 55 | www.turnhout.be*

VERDRONKEN LAND VAN
SAEFTINGHE ⚘
(126–127 C–D4) (*ᗈ J2–3*)

Poplar trees line the dykes and canals of the wonderfully calm polder landscape on the left bank of the Schelde. Extending behind a tall clay dyke, the 'Sunken Land' is a mudflat landscape covering 35 sq km/13.5 sq miles, populated by countless bird species (sea eagles amongst them). The sun breaking through the fog or clouds enhances the beauty of this site.

The *visitor centre (Emmaweg 4 | Emmadorp | tel. 0031 114 63 31 10 | j.neve@hetzeeuwselandschap.nl) has* an informative exhibition. The centre also organises guided tours (5 euros, booking required). *Access via the E34 Antwerp–Knokke, exit Kieldrecht, from there towards Nieuw-Namen and Emmadorp | www.saeftinghe.be*

MECHELEN

(127 E6) (*ᗈ L5*) **Mechelen welcomes visitors with young, multicultural vibes. Several colleges of higher education have settled in the town (pop. 76,000) – as well as immigrants commuting to Antwerp and Brussels for work.**

The tall tower of the monumental late Gothic cathedral, flying the Belgian tricolour, watches over everything: Mechelen is the residence of the cardinal archbishop, and in the early 16th century Mechelen was the capital of the Netherlands. Many monuments from this glorious era have been preserved.

SIGHTSEEING

BEGIJNHOF

All that is left of this small beguinage is the late Gothic *Sint-Katelijnekerk*, while the big beguinage on the other side of Katelijnestraat preserves the *Sint-Alexius* church, a Baroque gem which counted with the involvement of local master Lucas Fayd'herbe.

HOF VAN SAVOYE

Mechelen-born architect Rombout Keldermans – a star of his time who worked all over Flanders – created this Renaissance palace for Margaret of Austria, the widow of the Duke of Savoy. A well-educated ruler who governed the Netherlands from 1507 to 1530), she preferred tranquil Mechelen to the capital Brussels. Today, the palace houses the courts, and the courtyard is accessible to the public free of charge. *Keizerstraat*

KAZERNE DOSSIN

This museum in a former barracks documents the history of Jews and exiles before Germany's occupation of Belgium, persecution from 1940 onwards, the deportations to Auschwitz from this barracks and fierce resistance to the Nazis. *Thu–Tue 10am–5pm, closed on Jewish holidays | admission 10 euros | Goswin de Stassartstraat 153 | www.cicb.be*

INSIDER TIP KONINKLIJKE MANUFACTUUR DE WIT

Inside the refuge of the monks of Tongerlo dating back to 1484, the De Wit manufacture exhibits precious tapestries, restores splendid specimens from all over the world, and weaves modern creations too. *Visit and guided tour Sat 10.30am | admission 6 euros | Schoutetstraat 7 | tel. 015 20 29 05 | www.dewit.be*

Stylistic mix from Gothic to neo-Gothic: the Stadhuis of Mechelen

ONZE-LIEVE-VROUW-OVER-DE-DIJLE
This smaller version of the cathedral was commissioned by the powerful fishers' guild, who in the 17th century also splashed out on the Rubens triptych 'The Miraculous Catch of Fish'. *April–Oct Tue–Sun 1.30–5.30pm, Nov–March Tue–Sun 1.30–4.30pm | free admission | Onze-Lieve-Vrouwestraat*

admission, and free chairs in the garden of the A. Spinoy arts centre opposite the cathedral

STADHUIS
Mechelen's town hall consists of a stylistic mix from various centuries: the sturdy central part was planned in the early 14th century as a cloth hall with belfry,

Onze-Lieve-Vrouw-over-de-Dijle: the altarpiece 'Miraculous Catch of Fish' by Peter Paul Rubens

SINT-ROMBOUTSKATHEDRAAL ⭐ ⋇
The harmonious late Gothic cathedral by Rombout Keldermans is the icon of the city. Visible from afar, the tower only ended up being 97 m/318 ft high, instead of the planned 167 m/548 ft. *Easter–Oct Tue–Sun 10am–6pm | admission 7 euros.* The seat of the cardinal archbishop is blessed with the sound of two ● carillons. The city ringer and guests who have studied at Mechelen's royal ringing school play here on a regular basis. *Short ring Mon and Sat 11.30am, Sun 3pm, concerts June–Sept 8.30pm | free*

yet never completed. In the 17th century, the belfry was given a roof and turrets, the smaller right-hand wing a Dutch gable. The so-called *Paleisvleugel* (palace wing) on the left-hand corner was completed in 1911 in the neo-Gothic style.

STEDELIJK MUSEUM HOF VAN BUSLEYDEN
The museum displays numerous masterpieces of local crafts in the Renaissance palace of a wealthy humanist, embossed gilded leather tapestries, cabinet armoires, tapestries and smaller carillons

in particular. *Closed until 2015 for renovation | De Merodestraat 65–67*

INSIDER**TIP** GRAND CAFÉ LAMOT

Welcoming brasserie at the trendy fish market, fabulous terrace, and excellent breakfast. *Daily | Beethovenstraat 8/10 | tel. 015 20 95 30 | www.grandcafelamot. be | Budget*

D'HOOGH

Traditional meeting place, local specialities (asparagus). *Closed Sat lunchtime, Sun evening and Mon | Grote Markt 19 | tel. 015 21 75 53 | www.dhoogrestaurant. be | Expensive*

HOTEL CAROLUS

Original hotel in the buildings of the old *Het Anker* brewery. Quiet rooms with a view of the Begijnhof and an in-house brasserie. *22 rooms | Guido Gezellelaan 49 | tel. 015 28 71 41 | www.hotelcarolus. be | Budget*

HOTEL VÉ

Design hotel in a former smokehouse on the fish market. Very friendly service. *36 rooms | Vismarkt 14 | tel. 015 20 07 55 | www.hotelve.com | Moderate–Expensive*

Toerisme Mechelen | Hallestraat 2–4 | tel. 015 29 76 55 | www.inenuitmechelen.be

WESTERLO (130 B3–4) *(M N5)*

28 km/17 miles northeast of Mechelen, this neat little town (pop. 21,500) nestles in greenery. Visit the *Renaissance* moated castle of De Mérode, as well as – in the Tongerlo part of town, amongst fields and forests – the immense cloister of the *Norbertine abbey Tongerlo (guided tours April–Oct Sun 2.30pm | admission 1.50 euros | www.tongerlo.org)*, founded in 1130, with its old estate buildings and a white neo-Gothic church. The main attraction in the elegant neoclassical *Abtspalais Museum (daily 2–5pm | admission 3 euros) |* is a copy on canvas of Leonardo da Vinci's fresco 'The Last Supper'.

A straight-as-a-die country road leading through forests connects Tongerlo with the ★ *Abdij van Averbode (Mon–Sat 7.30–11.30am and 1.30–5.45pm, Sun 7.30–10.30am | www.abdijaverbode.be)*, also founded in 1130 by Norbertine monks.

The harmonious courtyard and the magnificent Baroque church erected on a cross-shaped plan with its fine wood carvings, marble sculptures and altars, and organs make Averbode the most beautiful abbey in all of Flanders. And the place has more to offer: in the outbuildings, the monks' publishing house prints comics and children's books.

LIMBURG

Amongst the provinces of Flanders, Limburg is the green one. In the flat north, expansive pine and birch forests extend across the poor sandy soils of the landscape called Kempen.

Extensive heathland alternates with tranquil lakes. Canals lead to the North Sea from the Maas, which forms the border with the Netherlands. In contrast, the hilly south, called Haspengouw, is the country's granary, orchard and pasture country, thanks to rich loess soils, flanked by oak trees, poplars and linden trees and criss-crossed by streams. In the centre, around Genk, you'll find an industrial area where coal was mined from 1901 until the closure of the last mine in 1992. Economic restructuring is only happening slowly here. This old area of

settlement for Celts, Romans and Franks has a fitting saying: 'Every village in Limburg has its baron.' Today still, strong moated castles, elegant manors and stately farm estates – some open to agritourism – belong to the descendants of old noble dynasties. In April, the Haspengouw turns into fairy-tale country when the apple, pear and cherry trees are in flower.

In this area belonging to the prince-bishopric of Liège, towns and cities played no major role, which explains their small size. To make up for this, Oud-Rekem emerged as the winner of a country-wide competition to find the prettiest village in Flanders. This compactness and the Limburgers' laid-back friendly temperament make this province so attractive.

Photo: Fruit trees in the Haspengouw

Flower power in the Roman Maasland: Limburg is a wonderful region for cycling and water sports

HASSELT

(130 C5) *(ɯ P–Q6)* **The modern and trendy provincial capital is also its biggest town (pop. 68,000).**

The thousands of young people studying at the university and several colleges of higher education enliven dozens of cafés, pubs and restaurants. The mostly pedestrianised town centre encourages vibrant life on streets and squares. Small buses commute for free to the car parks on the ring road. The *Pukkelpop rock festival in late* August is known beyond the region's borders.

NATIONAAL JENEVERMUSEUM

In the 19th century Hasselt had dozens of genever distilleries. The museum provides an introduction to the production and social history of the drink and serves every visitor with a *borreltje* in its pub. *April–Oct Tue–Sun 10am–5pm, Nov–*

March Tue–Fri 10am–5pm, Sat/Sun 1–5pm | admission 4.50 euros | Witte Nonnenstraat 19 | www.jenevermuseum.be

SINT-QUINTINUSKATHEDRAAL

The oldest church in town was elevated to the rank of cathedral in 1967. The beautifully restored interior of the church boasts a 15th-century triumphal cross

rior is adorned with ornate Baroque altars. *Daily 8am–6pm | Kapelstraat*

FOOD & DRINK

AUGUSTINA

Welcoming brasserie serving typically Belgian fare, including menus for children, in Art Nouveau ambience. There is

The town centre of Hasselt is a peaceful spot for strolling and shopping

and the tower houses a glockenspiel museum. *Daily 8am–6pm | Vismarkt/Fruitmarkt*

VIRGA-JESSE-BASILIEK

The Virgin Mary is particularly revered in Hasselt. Legend has it that in 1867 a sculpture of the smiling Madonna kept away a cattle disease. Since then it has been carried through the town every seven years (the next procession is scheduled for 2017). The basilica's inte-

a terrace too. *Daily | Leopoldsplein 23 | tel. 011 24 16 98 | www.augustina.be | Budget*

CAFÉ CONTRAST

From breakfast to late-night supper, solid Belgian dishes are served here. Atmospheric courtyard. *Daily | Badderijstraat 14 | tel. 011 23 67 06 | Budget*

VOUS LÉ VOUS ☺

Seasonal vegetables and herbs sourced in the region form the basis for creative dishes. And this is not only a place for eating well: in this modernised farmhouse on the edge of town, five rooms are available for a longer stay. *Closed Sun/Mon | Wimmertingenstraat 76 | tel. 011 74 81 85 | www.vouslevous.be | Moderate*

SHOPPING

Hasselt's town centre is the shopping centre of the province: *Demerstraat, Hoogstraat, Koning Albertstraat* and *Maastrichterstraat* appeal to the more budget-conscious shoppers, whereas *Kapelstraat, Aldestraat* and *Lombaardstraat* boast chic fashion boutiques and design stores.

STIJN HELSEN

This is the name of the local fashion wonder boy, who learned his trade with Giorgio Armani and Vivienne Westwood. Helsen first presents his clever clothing in his own boutique. *Kapelstraat 32 | www. stijnhelsen.be*

ENTERTAINMENT

MEGADISCOTHEEK VERSUZ

A happening club by the port; don't forget to enquire about the current dress code before setting off. *Mon, Thu, Sat from 10pm | Slachthuiskaai 6 | www. versuz.be*

INSIDER TIP MUZIEK-O-DROOM

Top centre for young experimental pop music. *Mon–Fri 4–11.30pm, Sat 9.30am–7pm | Bootstraat 9 | www.muziekodroom.be*

WHERE TO STAY

HOTEL PAX

Central location on the lively market square, with simply furnished rooms. *9 rooms | Grote Markt 16 | tel. 011 22 38 75 | www.hotelpax.be | Budget*

INFORMATION

Toerisme Hasselt | Lombaardstraat 3 | tel. 011 23 95 42 | www.hasselt.be

WHERE TO GO

BOCHOLT (131 D3) (Ø R4)

Situated 37 km/23 miles northeast of Hasselt, this town of 11,000 inhabitants is a stronghold of gun clubs (shooting festivals are held in July).

Worth seeing are the late Gothic *Sint Laurentiuskerk* and the huge INSIDER TIP *Brewery Museum (Bocholter Brouwerijmuseum | July/Aug daily 1–6pm | admission 5 euros | Dorpsstraat 53 | www.bocholterbrouwerijmuseum.be),* exhibiting a great range of equipment from the 18th to 20th centuries.

Gourmets flock to the nearby *Kaasmakerij Catharinadal* dairy *(Catharinadal 5 | Hamont-Achel | tel. 011 64 13 09 | www. catharinadal.be)*. This specialist cheese

MARCO POLO HIGHLIGHTS

⭐ **Landcommanderij Alden-Biesen**
One of the imposing castles with which the Teutonic Knights demonstrated their power → p. 88

⭐ **Gallo-Romeins Museum**
Modern setting for ancient gold and silver – in Tongeren → p. 89

⭐ **Onze-Lieve-Vrouwebasiliek**
Splendid Gothic church filled with art treasures in Tongeren → p. 90

⭐ **Sint-Truiden**
Cheerful Rococo architecture in the centre of flowering orchards → p. 91

shop supplies its varied products to Belgian's royal family.

LANDCOMMANDERIJ ALDEN-BIESEN
⭐ (131 D5) (𝕄 Q7)
This imposing moated castle 20 km/12 miles southeast of Hasselt was once the

MAASEIK (131 E3) (𝕄 S5)
This town 33 km/21 miles northeast of Hasselt (pop. 23,000) is an Eldorado for all water sports aficionados. There is a large marina *(Marec CVBA | Maasdijk | Kinrooi-Ophoven | tel. 089 56 75 03 | www.marec.be)* and a kayak club *(De Oeter |*

Gardens and parks surround the castle of Alden-Biesen, a former bastion of the Teutonic Knights

seat of the Teutonic Knights, and its ornate halls present the order's history. Hiking trails lead through the beautifully laid-out gardens and parks. There are also regular concerts of classical music. Welcoming inn. *Easter–Oct daily 10am–6pm, Nov/Dec and Feb–Easter Tue–Sun 10am–5pm | admission to castle and gardens 3 euros | Kasteelstraat 6 | Rijkhoven-Bilzen | tel. 089 51 93 93 | www.alden-biesen.be*

Ophovenstraat 135 | Maaseik-Neeroeteren | tel. 011 66 38 87 | www.oeter.be) with a hiring facility. Water skiing and speedboating are also on offer *(Marec Heerenlaak | Heerenlaakweg 100 | Maaseik | tel. 089 56 75 03 | www.marec.be)*, as well as sailing and windsurfing *(Sporta Beachclub | Heerenlaakweg 68 | Maaseik | tel. 089 56 77 61 | www.sporta.be)*.

On the market square and in the streets running off it, numerous restaurant are to be found. Art lovers will appreciate a look at the precious objects in the neo-Gothic *Sint-Catharinakerk* and the Rococo interior of the *Sint-Jacobskerk*, as well as the Romanesque *Sint-Annakerk*. *Information: Toerisme Maaseik | Markt 1 | tel. 089 81 92 90 | www.maaseik.be*

NATIONAAL PARK HOGE KEMPEN ☺
(131 D–E 4–5) (*ⓜ R5–6*)

33 km/21 miles east of Hasselt, the only national park in Flanders boasts 57.5 sq km/22 sq miles of pine forests, expanses of heather, lakes and greened coal dumps, featuring beautiful hiking and biking trails. The best way to get to know the area's rich flora and fauna is a free guided ● ranger tour. Visitor centre and cafeteria in the *Pietersheim moated castle (April–Oct Tue–Fri 10am–3.45pm, Sat/Sun 10am–4.45pm, Nov–March Fri–Sun 10am–4.45pm | Waterstraat | Lanaken | tel. 089 71 21 20 | www.nationaalpark.be)*.

In the immediate vicinity, the elegant *Hostellerie La Butte aux Bois (41 rooms | Paal-steenlaan 90 | Lanaken | tel. 089 73 97 70 | www.labutteauxbois.be | Moderate)* includes a large park on the forest edge, a gourmet restaurant, a friendly brasserie serving Limburg specialities, and the ● *Aquamarijn spa,* whose specialities include summer treatments and massages in the aromatic gardens.

TONGEREN

(131 D6) (*ⓜ Q7*) Tongeren (pop. 30,000) is a cosy provincial town – even on a Sunday, when traders and visitors flock to the flea and antique market in Flanders' oldest settlement.

In 54 BC, the Celtic Eburones under their leader Ambiorix – his monument stands on the market square – defeated Caesar's army. A year later they accept Roman rule after all, and *Atuatuca Tungrorum* rose to be a major town on the trade and army route from Cologne to Boulogne and Paris. Most of the Tongeren as it is today was built after the Second World War.

SIGHTSEEING

GALLO-ROMEINS MUSEUM ★

This elegant new building, built by the Limburg star architect Alfredo De Gregorio using only the finest Belgian stone, holds precious finds from the Celtic, Roman and Merovingian eras. Pleasant cafeteria. *Mon noon–5pm, Tue–Fri 9am–5pm, Sat/Sun 10am–6pm | admission 7 euros | Kielenstraat 15 | www.gallromeins museum.be*

MOERENPOORT ✄

History becomes alive in the striking city gate dating back to 1379. The crenella-

LOW BUDGET

▶ Tongeren offers free bikes (deposit 10 euros). *Toerisme Tongeren in the town centre*

▶ Discover a large selection of inexpensive accommodation on farms at *www.hoevetoerisme.be*. One agency for holiday apartments is *www.belvilla.de.*

▶ Toerisme Limburg offers the *Limburgpas*. Valid for one year (and for up to four people), the pass entitles the bearer to substantial discounts on admission fees to museums, churches and attractions. *Available from tourism offices and hotels*

tions of the gate offer panoramic views of the city and surroundings. *May–Sept Sat/Sun 11am–5pm | admission 1 euro | corner of Leopoldwal/Kastanjewal*

ONZE LIEVE VROUWEBASILIEK ★

Below the impressive Basilica of Our Lady, remains of a 4th-century church are a reminder of Tongeren's brief spell as a

BLANCKAERT

The best patisserie in town, serving snacks and brunch too. *Closed Mon | Maastrichterstraat 62 | Budget*

BRASSERIE BAZILIK

Friendly eatery across several floors and a pleasant terrace next to the basilica.

Tower of the Basilica of Our Lady and the monument to the Celtic king Ambiorix in Tongeren

bishopric. The Romanesque cloisters of a monastery were added later. The importance of the church is evidenced by precious artworks such as the large carved altar and the triumphal cross in the choir, the precious ivories and reliquary shrines in the treasury. There are regular organ and glockenspiel concerts in the basilica. *Daily 9am–5pm, treasury April–Sept daily 10am–noon and 1.30–5pm | admission 2.50 euros | Grote Markt*

Good food, kids' dishes, good selection of Limburg beers and wines. Friendly service. Open 10am–midnight. *Daily | Kloosterstraat 1–3 | tel. 012 21 33 24 | www.bazilik.be | Budget*

DE MIJLPAAL

Modern ambience for seasonal cuisine, using herbs from their own garden. *Closed Thu | Sint-Truiderstraat 25 | tel. 012 26 42 77 | www.demijlpaal.org | Moderate*

SHOPPING

350 to 400 traders take part in the *flea and antiques market (Sun 6am–1pm | Veemarkt | Leopoldswal)*.

WHERE TO STAY

INSIDER TIP ▶ **HOTEL EBURON**

Top designers from Limburg have styled a former hospice into an attractive hotel. Spacious, light-flooded rooms with avant-garde bathroom areas, fab wine bar, friendly courtyard. The ℳ terrace of the breakfast room offers fine views. The antiques market happens right outside the front door. *52 rooms | De Schiervelstraat 10 | tel. 012 23 01 99 | www.eburon hotel.be | Moderate–Expensive*

VILLA ESPERANZA

Classy bed & breakfast on the edge of town. The rooms in this villa, built in 1900, are very spacious and elegant. *3 rooms | Bilzersteenweg 155 | tel. 012 23 12 22 | www.villaesperanza.be | Moderate*

INFORMATION

Toerisme Tongeren | Stadhuisplein 9 | tel. 012 39 02 55 | www.tongeren.be

WHERE TO GO

BORGLOON
(130 C5–6) (*∅ Q7*)

This pretty little old town neat (pop. 10,000, 10 km/6 miles west of Tongeren) occupies a hill amidst the Haspengouw's seemingly endless orchards and used to be the ancestral seat of the dukes of Loon. Discover the elegant *Renaissance town hall,* the imposing Romanesque ℳ *Sint-Odolfuskerk,* with fine views of the Haspengouw from the square in front of the church.

SINT-TRUIDEN ⭐ (130 C5) (*∅ P7*)

20 km/12 miles west of Tongeren, this neat centre of fruit growing (pop. 36,000) emerged in the 7th century around the *Sint Trudo Abbey* – the ensemble of buildings on the market square that today is a boarding school. Worth seeing are the *Academiezaal* and the *Keizerzaal,* furnished in the Rococo style *(April–Oct Sat/Sun 2–5pm | free admission)*. The ℳ tower *(April–Sept Tue–Sun 10am–5pm, Oct–March Tue–Sun 10am–4pm | admission 3 euros)* of the abbey commands fabulous views.

Another instance of the exuberant Rococo style is the *town hall* on the extensive market square. The neighbouring Gothic *Onze Lieve Vrouw Hemelvaartkerk* has precious woodcarvings and a *treasury* filled to overflowing *(Sat/Sun 2–5pm | free admission)*. Regular organ concerts are held inside the church. Only a stone's throw away, the *Minderbroederkerk (Minderbroedersplein)* possesses a gleaming Rococo interior.

The oldest *beguine church* in Flanders (1258) boasts vaulted wooden ceilings and medieval frescoes *(Begijnhof | April– Oct Tue–Fri 10am–12.30pm and 1.30– 5pm, Sat/Sun 1.30–5pm | free admission)*.

An excellent food option – in summer in the fresh air of a divine garden – is the *Aen de Kerck van Melveren* restaurant *(closed Mon/Wed evening, Sat lunchtime and Sun evening | Sint-Godfriedstraat 15–21 | tel. 011 68 39 65 | www.aende kerck.be | Moderate)*. Rustic bread-based fare is served in the traditional INSIDER TIP ▶ *Kerkom Brewery (April–Oct Tue, Nov–March closed Mon–Wed | Naamsesteenweg 469 | tel. 011 68 20 87 | www.brouwerijkerkom.be)*.

Information: Dienst Toerisme | Stadhuis | Grote Markt | tel. 011 70 18 18 | www. toerisme-sint-truiden.be

TRIPS & TOURS

The tours are marked in green in the road atlas,
pull-out map and on the back cover

1 BUCOLIC LANDSCAPES IN THE HASPENGOUW

At 55km/34 miles long, this bike tour describes a loop through the Haspengouw: to the Château de la Motte and the Rococo palace at Hex, to Borgloon and through the nature reserve along the Herkbach stream. The starting and end point is Sint-Truiden. *Dienst Toerisme* is the place to rent bikes *(8 euros per day, with child seat 9 euros | April–Sept daily 10am–6pm | Grote Markt 44 | bookings tel. 011 33 27 56)*. This is also where you can pick up a detailed map and the *Fietsinfo-boekje* (for 7.50 euros), which turn the route into child's play. All cycle paths are marked by blue signs, the crossings *(knooppunten)* are given precise locations. The tour described here runs via points *(knooppunten)* 134–168–169–161–163–159–158–157–156–151–152–153–148–149–171–189–135. For any information on this biker's paradise, see *www.toerismelimburg.be*.

In spring, the Haspengouw displays the fascinating splendour of millions of fruit-tree blossoms, in summer undulating cornfields and in the autumn the trees shimmer golden in the sun. All you need to do is cycle from point to point, partly on pedestrianised paths and usually on asphalt.

The map features the distances, ascents, restaurants, picnic spots, accommodation and sights, all described in the accompanying booklet. Along the paths

Photo: Rococo Château Hex in the Haspengouw

Lovely landscapes, castles and beer: cycle through the Haspengouw and around Ypres, and discover the Pajottenland

you'll find overview maps and information pillars. The Limburg network also offers a break-down service. Many hotels and bed & breakfasts are available to take your luggage on to the next stop-off point.

Blue signs bearing the inscription *Fietsroutennetwerk* take you from Grote Markt in the town centre of **Sint-Truiden** → p. 91 to *knooppunt 134*. From there you'll be cycling through a flat landscape, flanked by endless ranks of apple and pear trees. Cornfields, cattle pastures

and small chapels with saints' statues provide diversion, and the view sweeps into the distance.

Between *no. 168* and *no. 161*, the path runs straight as a die, like an old Roman military road. Afterwards, you enter a soft valley landscape, the path winds through narrow passes, uphill, downhill... Brooks and ponds are host to many ducks and geese, the wetlands resound to the rustling of poplars and willows. You cycle through pretty villages with stately farms and churches, past moated castles and pleasure palaces. Château de la Motte has a café where cyclists are welcome. In the park are benches to recover on, as well as a playground. Take a moment's rest in Heks. On a hill on the edge of the village you'll discover the vermilion Rococo Château Hex *(www. hex.be)* – in June and September the castle hosts a INSIDER TIP festival of rare plants, roses and kitchen gardens.

At *knooppunt 151* it's worth your while taking a quick detour to Borgloon → p. 91. At the edge of town lies the prim white-washed *Cistercian abbey Marienlof Colen* with an ancient blacksmith's forge and its *Museum of Fruit Cultivation* (Fr*uitstreekmuseum* | Tue–Sat 2–5pm, Sun 3–5pm | admission 1.25 euros | Colenstraat).

From *knooppunt 153* you'll be cycling through the lovely nature reserve around the Herkbach and past protected slopes growing vines. Past *no. 149* it's uphill once more, and the views range free again.

From *no. 189* blue signs with *Centrum* will direct you back to the starting point at Sint-Truiden.

2 CASTLES, BEER AND BRUEGHEL IN WESTERN BRABANT

This day-long tour covering 90 km/56 miles leads through western Brabant. The hilly Pajottenland, or Payottenland, which inspired the painter Pieter Bruegel, is home to the special gueuze beer. The tour starts from Beersel Castle and goes via Enghien Castle to the quiet countryside around Vollezele. Gaasbeek Castle is followed by the Gothic churches of Ternat, Asse and Merchtem. Near the Diepensteyn moated castle, the Palm brewery still breeds Old Brabant draught horses. For this tour, involving small side roads, a detailed map is a good investment.

Right behind exit no. 19 of the E19 Brussels–Paris motorway appears the medieval moated castle of Beersel *(March–Nov Tue–Sun 10am–12 noon and 2–6pm, Nov/Dec, Feb Sat/Sun 10am–12 noon and 2–5pm | admission 2.50 euros | Lotsestraat 65)*. Opposite the church you'll find the restaurant *3 Fonteinen (closed Tue/Wed | Herman Teirlinckplein 3 | tel. 02 3 31 06 52 | www.3fonteinen.be | Budget)*, with the old-fashioned gueuze brewery run by the Debelder family behind.

From Beersel, the *Hoogstraat* leads out to Alsemberg. Turn right at the traffic lights opposite the late Gothic church towards Halle – the high Gothic *Sint-Martinus church* with a highly revered sculpture of the Virgin Mary is worth a visit. Carry on across the fields via Beert, Den Daal and Bosstraat to Enghien (or Edingen: this little town lies at the language frontier with the German-speaking part of Belgium). A *Renaissance triumphal arch* is a reminder of the palace of the counts of Arenberg; what has remained is the splendid park with a collection of dahlias that has no equal in Europe (over 750 types).

The N255 will take you to Herne with its Romanesque church, then Vollezele, where you turn left at the church square in the direction of Congoberg. *Repingestraat* winds its way through the peaceful landscape at your feet. A field track leads to the old Leysbroek abbey estate *(Repingestraat 9)*, where sculptor Koenraad Tinel enjoys receiving visitors. Return to Vollezele village and on to the N255/N272 crossroads, and turn left there. Via Kester, Kestergat (cross the N28 there) and Elingen, the tour leads through soft hills to the Kasteel van Gaasbeek *(April–Oct Tue–Sun 10am–6pm, admission 7 euros | park 10am–8pm, admission free | www.kasteel vangaasbeek.be)*, a mighty medieval castle belonging to the counts of Brabant with precious artworks inside.

Via Goudveerdegem you arrive at **Wambeek** with its late Renaissance church, well worth a stop, as well as the traditional gueuze brewery *De Troch (Langestraat 20 | www.detroch.be)*. Now carry on via **Ternat**, **Asse** and **Merchtem** (with impressive churches) to **Steenhuffel**: the *Palm Brewery (Steenhuffeldorp 3)* is one of the oldest family-run breweries, brewing the special beers *Brugse Tripel* and *Rodenbach* alongside their light-coloured strong beer. Behind the old brewery, discover the **Diepensteyn moated castle**, the last important INSIDER TIP centre for breeding heavy Brabant draught horses *(visits can be arranged through Martine Devaux | tel. 052 31 74 14)*.

From Steenhuffel carry on to Wolvertem and onto the A12 to the motorway ring road. Following signs to Charleroi/Mons/Paris will take you back to Beersel.

3 TRAGIC BEAUTY IN THE HILLS AROUND YPRES

Covering 75 km/45 miles, this tour lasting one or two days mainly follows the 'Ypres Arc' of World War I. About one million soldiers died here. Ieper (Ypres) and the surrounding villages, fields and forests were completely destroyed – and reconstructed after 1918. Today, the attractions are peace, charm and culinary delights. This tour leads from the hop-growing town of Poperinge to the war cemeteries of Langemark, Tyne Cot and Buttes New British Cemetery. Past the Kemmelberg, Rodeberg and Mont Noir, the artists' village Watou awaits, offering delicious special beers.

The starting point is **Poperinge** → p. 43 with its pretty market square, three Gothic churches, and, as a foretaste of things to come, the Hops Museum. *Krombekerstraat* leads you out of town, past hop fields, to *De Lovie Castle.* At the end of the

Bulky from the outside, full of art inside: Kasteel van Gaasbeek in western Brabant

well-kept park turn right to the **Trappist abbey of Sint-Sixtus**. This is where the world's best beer is brewed; it would be a sin not to sample it in the *In de Vrede* hostelry. Well-signposted paths make a stroll through the forest an inviting proposition. The narrow road now leads to **Eikhoek**, where you cross the N321, then the N8. You're now on cycle path no. 74., winding ing, allowing visitors to sample the aromatic specialities in the restaurant. Following that, take's *Graventafelstraat* further uphill, and after 600 m/650 yards, turn right into *Tynecotstraat*. In the distance you can see the monumental white crescent created by Sir Herbert Baker in memory of nearly 35,000 British soldiers whose bodies were never

Memorial site and cemetery for victims of the First World War: Tyne Cot Cemetery

its way through fields and pastures, past farms and carp ponds to **Zuidschote**. Turn left at the church, in the direction of Diksmuide, approx. 300 m/350 yd further right to **Bikschote**. Pass the windmill and head for **Langemark**; there, behind the church fringed by linden trees, take a left for *German War Cemetery*. 44,324 soldiers were laid to rest here under oaks. Back in the village, drive straight on beyond the church in the direction of Zonnebeke. Crossing the N313 and carrying on for 2.5 km/1.5 miles turn left at the white **New Zealand Memorial**, to *De Oude Kaasmakerij (March–11 Nov daily 10am–5pm | admission 4 euros |'s Graventafelstraat 48a | Passendale | www. deoudekaasmakerij.be)*. Housed in a former cheese dairy, the museum provides an introduction to artisan cheese-mak-

found. In front, the well-kept ☆ **Tyne Cot Cemetery** holds 12,000 graves. From here you can see Ypres and further into the Heuvelland.

From Tyne Cot Cemetery, drive through a residential neighbourhood to the N303, turn right and once more right at the roundabout, towards **Zonnebeke**. At the church follow the sign to Ypres, turning left immediately beyond the castle park and driving straight on up the hill to *Polygon Wood*. In the area today covered by a romantic pine forest covered in ferns, you'll find **Buttes New British Cemetery**, arguably the region's most beautiful war cemetery. An obelisk above the former defensive wall acts as a reminder of the 5th Australian Division, a white colonnade for New Zealand soldiers who died here. The forest features waymarked hiking trails. The road at the forest edge leads to the *De Hoeve hostelry (closed Mon | Budget)*, where you can fortify yourself with rustic bread, pancakes and beer. Afterwards, drive left through the *Lotegatstraat* down the hill following the forest edge, taking a right at the first crossroads, crossing the motorway and straight ahead to the N8. There you take a left, and a right at the *obelisk for the 18th English Division* in the direction of Zillebeke. At the end of *Pappotstraat* turn left, some 100 m/100 yards on right again into *Kasteelhoekstraat*, to join a beautifully bucolic, undulating forest landscape.

Beyond the railway underpass, turn left towards Hollebeke. From the left-hand corner of the pretty church square, the bendy street branches off towards Wijtschate – where you follow, once again at the church square, the signs pointing to Kemmel. At the end of the splendid long avenue of linden trees you'll already spot the Kemmelberg hill.

Via the square of Kemmel village, drive steeply up the wooded hill and then along its eastern flank in the direction of Monteberg. The narrow road winds its way through the INSIDER TIP vineyards of the eponymous estate *(visits and wine tastings by appointment only | www.monteberg.be)* to Dranouter. At the church you'll find a signpot to the hotel restaurant ● 😊 *In de Wulf (closed Mon/Tue, as well as Wed and Sat lunch | Wulvestraat 1 | tel. 057 44 55 67 | www.indewulf.be | Expensive)*. In this rustic restaurant framed by softly rising fields, the most interesting chef working in Flanders today, Kobe Desramaults, creates exciting dishes prepared exclusively with local organic produce – including herbs, berries, flowers and mushrooms. You'll also be able to get to know Heuvelland wines. Nine comfortable rooms without TV or internet have a calming effect, and are the more recommended for the wonderful walks that Kobe can suggest.

In Dranouter, take the N322 to Loker, to enjoy a pastoral landscape. At the crossing behind the centre of town, take a left towards Rodeberg. At the end of this fairly touristy village cross the border to France and take the D318 to Mont Noir. Right inside the *Parc Départemental* you'll find the *Villa Marguerite Yourcenar,* which today welcomes European writers. From the extensive ☀️ park, travellers can enjoy fabulous views, which on a clear day can range all the way to the English Channel coast. Literary connoisseurs will also be able to recognise landscape in many passages from the collection of memoirs by the great writer Yourcenar, *How Many Years*.

Now drive downhill on the D318, at the roundabout taking the ☀️ D10 in the direction of Boeschèpe, with wonderful far-ranging views to Ypres, and on to L'Abeele, where you cross the N38 to arrive in the small Belgian village of Abele. At the end of a street lined by maple trees you'll find Watou. A monument dedicated to Hugo Claus on the village square proclaims that the well-known poetry and arts festival is held here in summer. The restaurants around the square with the Romanesque-Gothic church serve (and sell) INSIDER TIP over a dozen local beer specialities: Hommelbier, Kapittel, Sint-Bernardus, Yedeghemsche. To mop up the alcohol, we'd recommend a *hoppegalette* – a savoury pancake prepared with beer and hops extract – or a rustic bread with cheese or ham from Watou, to gather up strength for the last 8 km/5 miles through hop fields back to Poperinge.

Information: Dienst voor Toerisme | Sint-Laurentiusplein 1 | Kemmel-Heuvelland | tel. 057 45 04 55 | www.heuvelland.be

SPORTS & ACTIVITIES

Flanders borders the English Channel to the west and the Maas River to the east. The landscape is criss-crossed by countless canals, with a sophisticated system of locks connecting rivers big and small. The Flemish and the water are made for each other – with plenty of water sports to choose from. One true Flemish experience is a slow boat tour, allowing you to discover the countryside and cities from the water. The national sport in this flat country is cycling. Young people too will find ways to expend energy, skating for instance. Check out the whole range of sports at *www.spinonline.be*.

BOATING

Countless canals and waterways criss-cross flat Flanders. A pleasant way to get to know the country is a round trip aboard a boat. If you can't bring your own boat, you can hire one, at *Le Boat (www.leboat.com)* for instance in Nieuwpoort or in Ghent. Amateur skippers don't need a licence for a boat under 15 m (approx. 50ft). A detailed map of the Flemish waterways (8.50 euros) and a book *(Vaartboek,* 30 euros) with all the information you need (such as how to work the locks and moorings) are available from the west Flemish tourist board *Westtoer (www.westtoer.be)*.

COURSES

Information about how to make chocolates und courses even are available at the

Photo: Canal outside Damme

Outdoor is trendy: sailing and windsurfing, bike tours with the children, fine hiking trails – active holidaymakers will find a great choice in Flanders

● *Choco Center (course fee 30 or 40 euros | www.choco-story.be) of the Choco Story* chocolate museum in Bruges. In two hours you can learn to make your own chocs, in three how to create chocolate truffles. The museum provides a glimpse into the cultivation of various kinds of cocoa trees, the processing of the beans into chocolate and its triumphal progress from Mexico all over the globe. Also in Bruges, the *Kantcentrum* offers courses in lace-making, running over several days for beginners and advanced levels. *Fee 210 euros | www.kantcentrum.eu*

Varied cookery classes are available from *Mmmmh! (course fee 17–65 euros | www. mmmmh.be)* in Brussels or at *Vous Lé Vous (course fee 66–90 euros | www. foodbuilding.be)* in Hasselt.

CYCLING

The *Flandriens* have made sports history: cycling is the Flemish national sport – which translates into a well-maintained and signposted network of roads. Limburg and west Flanders each have a network of separate cycle paths. En route you'll find bike-friendly restaurants and accommodation (where on longer tours your luggage will be transported to the next stop for example). In Limburg even car service stations come equipped for bikes. The detailed maps cost 7.50 euros per province *(www.toerismelimburg.be | www.westtoer.be)*. Bikes can be hired from any major railway station from the *fietspunt*, in tourist areas even with children's seats or trailers for children (rental fee approx. 10 euros per day). Some hotels and guesthouse owners provide free bikes for their guests. Excellent information and links can be found at *www.rad flandern.com | www.vlaanderen-fietsland. be | www.fietsnet.be | www.fietsroute.org*

FISHING

The Flemish are passionate anglers, whether on canals, rivers or lakes, on their own or as part of a club. *Les bateaux Marcella (35–55 euros | tel. 059 32 00 72 | www.marcella.be)* in Oostende hit the high seas on a daily basis. For more information on clubs: *www.hengel sportbeurs.be.* What you will definitely need is a fishing permit *(visverlof)*, available from any post office, with the requisite rules and regulations, costing between 3.72 euros (children under 14 with a rod) to 45.86 euros.

HIKING

Over 3000 km/1900 miles of signposted hiking trails lead through Flanders' finest landscapes. Limburg and western Flanders have very well waymarked hiking trails and the relevant maps for shorter or longer tours *(www.toerismelimburg. be | www.westtoer.be)*. The Flemish network connects seamlessly with the GR network in Wallonia, France and the Netherlands *(Grote Route* or *Grande Randonnée | www.groteroutepaden.be)*.

A particularly intense experience is on offer along the 3km/1.8-mile long *Blote Voetepad (Easter–Oct daily 10am–7pm | admission 3 euros | Stalkerweg | Zutendaal | tel. 089 25 50 60 | www.lieteberg.be)* in the Hoge Kempen national park. The trail only allows barefoot walking across branches and stones, through grass and water and onto a viewing tower.

In the *Forêt de Soignes (Zonienwoud)*, stretching 50 sq km/19 sq miles from Brussels to Wallonia across a strip of Flanders, the environmental association *Natagora* regularly organises guided tours, for example to nesting sites of birds and bats. For more information: *www.natagora.be*

HORSERIDING

The coastal resorts in particular have riding stables and manèges, as well as waymarked riding trails through the countryside. Make sure you ask in advance whether and where horseriding is allowed on the beaches.

SWIMMING

The Flemish coast has 39 official swimming beaches: a round, blue-and-white sign showing waves, swimmers and blue 'B' means that the beach is safe and has lifeguards in season. A round red sign with a red 'B' and a red bar across tells you that the spot is dangerous and unsupervised. The sea is particularly treacherous around breakwaters and the entrances to ports. Last not least, watch out for the little triangular weather flag: when it's green, you may swim and practise water sports. When it's yellow, water sports are banned. When it's red, both swimming and water sports are banned.

The water quality of the swimming beaches is regularly checked. A sign showing a smiley means good water quality, a sign with a sad-looking emoticon bad; and if the smiley has a slash through it, the water is just about acceptable (for more information: *www.vmm.be*).

The inland provinces offer sports and leisure parks (Provinciaal Domein) in pretty landscapes, with a swimming lake or pool. Swimming in canals or rivers is not a good idea. The currents can be dangerous, and the waters heavily polluted.

TENNIS

Tennis is trendy. Wallonian crack Justine Henin and her Flemish equivalent Kim Clijsters reached top world rankings. The Flemings Xavier Malisse, Kristof Vliegen and Yanina Wickmayer as well as the Walloons David Goffin and Olivier Rochus are currently defending Belgium's tricolour on the courts. Most courts welcome guests. For more information on courts, prices and courses: *www.vtv.be*

WATER SPORTS

Sailors and windsurfers can indulge their sporting passion on the coast and in the Maasland in Limburg, as can speedboat and water skiers; the latter however have to stick to delimited and restricted areas and times, as well as strict safety regulations. On the North Sea coast, numerous clubs offer sailing and windsurfing courses. Beginners are best picking up the basics from *Inside-Outside (www.vvwinout. be)* in Oostende. Advanced sailors and surfers should contact *Vlaamse Zeezeil school (www.vvwnieuwpoort.be)* in Nieuwpoort. A major current trend is INSIDER TIP kitesurfing, sailing through the air from the water – the tricks can be learnt in Oostduinkerke (the only school: *www.kitesurfschool.be*). Particular fun can be had sand-yachting on the broad beaches of De Panne and Oostduinkerke where you'll find schools, which also rent out the sailing soapboxes *(www. strandzeilen.be)*.

Swish across the sandbank propelled by the North Sea wind: sand-yachting near De Panne

TRAVEL WITH KIDS

Flanders is very child-friendly indeed. In holiday resorts on the coast and in Limburg in particular, the little ones are well and truly spoilt.

A cot in the parents' room, a kiddies' menu or adapted dish form part of standard service. And the many exciting attractions ensure that boredom gets no look-in. For up-to-date online tips consult *www.agenda.be/kid*.

BRUGES AND WEST FLANDERS

MU.ZEE (124 B2) (*𝄞 C3–4*)

The museum for modern art in Oostende is well-known for its creative children's workshops. The kids may gather ideas in the museum and then implement their ideas. When they get stuck, knowledgeable help is at hand. Numbers are limited, so book ahead! *Wed 2–4pm, admission 4 euros | school holidays Mon–Fri 10am–6pm, admission 2.50 euros | Romestraat 11 | Oostende | www.muzee.be*

SEA LIFE MARINE PARK (124 C1) (*𝄞 D3*)

Watch North Sea crabs live in action! There are also 30 basins featuring hundreds of fish, and outdoors seals and penguins splash around. *July/Aug daily 10am–7pm, Easter–1 Nov daily 10am–6pm, Nov–Easter daily 10am–5pm | admission online purchase adults and children from 12 years 12 euros, children 3–11 years 10.50 euros (at the entrance 17 / 13.50 euros), under 3 years go free | Kon-*

Fun for kids on water and on dry land: interactive museums, farms and visits to the zoo leave no time to be bored

ing-Albert-I-laan 116 | Blankenberge | www.sealife.be

GHENT AND EAST FLANDERS

STEAM LOCOMOTIVE TRIPS

Vintage steam trains ply two routes: one leading through the Scheldeland from Dendermonde to Puurs (126–127 C–D6) (*J–K5*). The point of departure is the *Baasrode-Noord Station (Fabriekstraat)* with its railway tavern and specialised bookstore. The sheds house carriages and locomotives, and visitors are welcome to watch the restoration work in action (departure times and prices: *www.stoomtrein.be*). The second line with a large steam engine and old-fashioned carriages connects Maldegem with Eeklo (125 E2) (*E–F4*) (northwest of Ghent). In the railway museum in Maldegem (train station) rare steam machines on display (departure times and prices: *www.stoomcentrum.be*).

FLEMISH BRABANT

MUSÉE DES SCIENCES NATURELLES
(129 E–F2) *(Ⓜ L7)*

The biggest attraction of the Museum for Natural Sciences in Brussels are dinosaur skeletons up to 10m/33 ft long and 125 million years old! The wonders of the natural world are explained in a way that children can understand. There are regular changing exhibitions specifically with children in mind. The INSIDER TIP BiodiverCity section allows visitors to discover the modern interaction of flora, fauna and humans in the big city. Computers ask questions about personal lifestyle choices, simulating the consequences for biodiversity. There are also children's rooms with small cottages, animated films, and interactive games, as well as the *Paleo Lab,* where children can play at being palaeontologists. *Tue–Fri 9.30am–5pm, Sat/Sun 10am–6pm, in the school holidays Tue–Sun 10am–6pm | admission adults 7 euros, children 6–17 years of age 4.50 euros, under 6 free, PaleoLab supplement 2 euros | www.sciencesnaturelles.be | Rue Vautier 29 | buses 20, 59, 80*

OCÉADE (129 E–F2) *(Ⓜ K6)*

Tropical fun in Brussels at a water park with exciting flumes. There are several games that children can play under supervision, while the parents may take advantage of the sauna or the hammam. *Wed–Fri 10am–4pm, Sat/Sun 10am–9pm | admission children up to 1.15m/3 ft 9 inches go free, 1.15–1.30 m 14.50 euros, over 1.30m/4 ft 3 inches and adults 17.50 euros | Boulevard du Centenaire/Bruparck | Metro Heizel | www.oceade.be*

ANTWERP

KIDS' RESTAURANT (127 D–E 4–5) *(Ⓜ L4)*

Here children learn to cook tasty healthy food, in a playful way – from finger food to cakes, Flemish as well as Mediterranean. *Grote Markt 29 | Antwerp | tel. mobile 0475 65 57 85 | www.artofchildren.be*

SPEELGOEDMUSEUM (127 E6) *(Ⓜ L5)*

This huge interactive toy museum in Mechelen brings together children's dreams from all eras and all around the globe. There is a play area, and you can hold picnics in the cafeteria. *Tue–Sun 10am–5pm | admission adults and children from 12 years upwards 8 euros, children under 12 5.50 euros | Nekkerspoel 21 | www.speelgoedmuseum.be*

TECHNOPOLIS (127 E6) *(Ⓜ L5)*

Interactive centre covering all aspects of natural sciences and technology, as well as the environment, health, and new media. The experiments may be repeated online. *Daily 9.30am–5pm | admission adults 12 euros, children 3–11 years of age 9.50 euros, under 3 free | Technologielaan Mechelen | www.technopolis.be*

ZOO ★ (127 D–E 4–5) *(Ⓜ L4)*

Antwerp's zoo was founded in 1843 and became one of the largest in Europe with the colonisation of the Congo (featuring 950 species). Alongside many buildings dating back to the Belle Époque, you'll find attractions such as a planetarium, children's playground and conservatory. Between September and March guided tours take visitors backstage. *Nov–Feb daily 10am–4.45pm, March, April, Oct daily 10am–5.30pm, May, June, Sept daily 10am–6pm, July/Aug daily 10am–7pm | admission adults 22 euros, children 3–17 years 17 euros, under 3 free of charge | Koningin Astridplein 26 (next to the central railway station) | www.zooantwerpen.be*

LIMBURG

OPEN-AIR MUSEUM BOKRIJK
(131 D4) *(Ⓜ Q6)*

This museum recreates entire town neighbourhoods and villages from all the Flemish provinces, showing a true-to-life representation of life in bygone times, whether of craftsmen or pastors. Some

used to transport coal, now leads to the viewing tower. Another great option is a trip on the *Railbike (April–Nov Sat/Sun and in the school holidays 9.30 and 11.30am | per rail bike 20 euros | Stationstraat 124 | As | www.railbikelimburg.be)* on the As–Eisden route. Smaller children will have a fabulous time on the *Pietersheim Children's Farm (daily April–Oct*

Exciting discoveries for rangers big and small in Hoge Kempen national park

children will love the huge playground. *April–Sept Tue–Sun 10am–6pm | admission 3–26 years of age 1 euro, under 3 years of age free of charge, adults over 26 July/Aug 10 euros (otherwise 7 euros) | Het Domein Bok-rijk | Park Midden-Limburg | Genk | www.bokrijk.be*

NATIONAAL PARK HOGE KEMPEN
(131 D–E 4–5) *(Ⓜ R6)*

The national park puts on exciting activities for children There's a course where they are trained to be **INSIDER TIP** Junior Rangers *(costing 2 euros, or 5 euros for the entire family | tel. 089 62 28 67 | www.lieteberg.be).*

A *narrow-gauge railway (May–Oct Wed 2pm, Sat/Sun 2, 3 and 4pm | admission 3 euros, family ticket 8 euros | Stationstraat 124 | As | www.stationas.be),* which

8am–9pm, Nov–March 8am–6pm | admission free *| Neerharenweg 12 | Lanaken | www.pietersheim.be)* with many chickens and rabbits, a huge play area and the 3km/1.8-mile long *Kabouterpad* ('Dwarves' Trail').

GLORIOUS COUNTRYSIDE
(131 D6) *(Ⓜ Q7)*

Farm holidays are a great experience for city kids, especially if they are allowed to lend a hand, as at the *Ruttermolen (2 rooms. | Ruttersmolenstraat 20 | Tongeren | tel. 012 24 16 24 | www.ruttermolen.be | Budget),* where cereals are ground and used for baking bread. Another attraction are bikes with trailers for the little ones, and cycle trails through fields and forests. *www.hoevetoerisme.be | www.toerismeliburg.be*

FESTIVALS & EVENTS

PUBLIC HOLIDAYS

1 Jan New Year; **Easter Monday; 1 May** Labour Day; **Ascension Day; Whitsun Monday; 21 July** Belgian National Holiday; **15 Aug** Assumption of the Virgin Mary; **1 Nov** All Saints; **11 Nov** Armistice 1918; **25 and 26 Dec** Christmas

FESTIVALS & EVENTS

JANUARY

▶ *Brafa:* Belgium's chic top antiquities fair in Brussels (Tour et Taxis) is attended by the leading Flemish dealers (end of the month). *www.brafa.be*

▶ INSIDERTIP *Lichtfeest:* for three nights running, renowned light designers turn Ghent into a fairy-tale city (second half of the month).

FEBRUARY/MARCH

▶ *Carnival:* two processions in the eastern Flemish town of Aalst, numerous balls in Limburg province

MARCH/APRIL

▶ *Ronde van Vlaanderen:* Legendary tough cycle race (end of March/early April)

APRIL

▶ ● *Floralien:* beautiful flower arrangements by the best growers and arrangers, who bring out the best in the local azaleas and begonias. At the ICC in Ghent (every five years, next show 2015). *www.floralien.be*

MAY/JUNE

▶ *Holy Blood Procession:* respected citizens of Bruges carry a relic through the city, with a colourful accompaniment (Ascension Day).

JUNE

▶ *Rock Werchter:* this seminal rock and pop festival featuring young bands and visitors rings in the festival season on the meadows outside Leuven (last weekend of month). *www.rockwerchter.be*

JULY

▶ ● *Gentse Feesten:* ten-day popular fair in Ghent with plenty of music and street performers, partying across the entire city and evening lights display (end of the month). All concerts and performances are free. *www.gentsefeesten.be*

▶ *Sfinks Festival:* meet-up of the best names in world music in the Boechout park outside Antwerp. *www.sfinks.be*

Arts and music non-stop: festivals, fairs, processions – there's always something going on somewhere in Flanders

JULY/AUGUST

▶ *Zomer van Antwerpen:* dance, music and poetic circus on the banks of the Schelde (up to end of Aug). *www.zva.be*

▶ *MAfestival:* leading festival for ancient music in Bruges, competitions for harpsichord and organ, amongst other instruments (ten days early Aug). INSIDER TIP preliminaries, semi-finals and ten free fringe concerts by young ensembles. *www.mafestival.be*

JULY–SEPTEMBER

▶ *Zandskulpturenfestival* in Blankenberge: monumental sand art on the beach, with a different theme every year

AUGUST

▶ *Jazz Middelheim:* Hip meeting in the Sculpture Park near Antwerp

▶ *Laus polyphoniae:* one-week festival for ancient music in Antwerp's Augustinuskerk, taking an in-depth look at an individual composer (second half of the month). *www.festivalvanvlaanderen-antwerpen.be*

▶ *Reiefeest* in Bruges: splendidly staged episodes from the city's history (canals and castle square, every three years: 2014, 2017). *www.reiefeest.be*

SEPTEMBER

▶ *Open Monumentendag:* hundreds of monuments are open to the public for the day, with a different theme every year.

OCTOBER

▶ *Biennale Interieur:* fair for modern design in Kortrijk (in even-numbered years, next in 2014). *www.interieur.be*

NOVEMBER

▶ *Lineart:* leading fair for modern and contemporary art and graphic design in Ghent (Flanders' Expo). *www.lineart.be*

DECEMBER

▶ ● *Kerststallen:* nativity scenes with life-sized figures are set up around Turnhout, often featuring real animals in authentic regional stables.

LINKS, BLOGS, APPS & MORE

LINKS

▶ www.marco-polo.com See the page on Brussels for lots of information about the Belgian capital

▶ www.bierebel.com Every year, new beers produced by microbreweries come onto the Belgian market. Find all the information you need here

▶ www.cafebabel.com Made by young Europeans, this magazine looks at European issues, but also reports on day-to-day life in Brussels and other towns and cities

▶ www.flanderninfo.be The homepage of public-service broadcaster VRT offers a good overview of current affairs. Numerous videos on the country and its people, as well as a selection of miscellaneous subjects

▶ www.monarchie.be The official homepage of the Belgian royal family offers royalty fans all the information on the history and current members of the Belgian dynasty

NETWORKS

▶ www.belgiancoastgreeters.com Residents of the Belgian coast show their resorts; visitors are given the opportunity to leave comments later on

▶ www.streetpage.be Social network run by the inhabitants of various neighbourhoods, with potentially very useful offers and tips

▶ www.spottedbylocals.com Locals provide hot tips for Antwerp, Ghent and Brussels

▶ www.toursbylocals.com The locals leading tours through Antwerp, Bruges, Ghent or the battlefields of the First World War are carefully selected, with the users rating their quality

▶ www.apen.be/videos-antwerpen Nice videos from and about Antwerp

Regardless of whether you are still preparing your trip or already in Flanders: these addresses will provide you with more information, videos and networks to make your holiday even more enjoyable.

VIDEOS, STREAMS & PODCASTS

▶ www.meteobelgie.be Dozens of webcams show the weather in all towns, cities and regions of Belgium

▶ www.mnm.be Pop channel with live streaming, podcast and videos

▶ www.worbz.com Belgian site promoting fantastic young photographic art, with an online pinboard where users may publish their own photographs

▶ www.stubru.be Cult programme of public broadcaster VRT, original, slightly alternative music selection. Live streaming, podcast und Videos

BLOGS & FORUMS

▶ www.cyclechic.be Smart blog, with plenty of tips and fun pictures made by cyclists for cyclists, particularly useful for the cities

▶ www.ilovebelgium.be Stijn and Tom present their personal selection of (mainly arty) trends, allowing space for comments

▶ www.theflemishprimitives.com The latest news from and about Flanders' avantgarde chefs, including fabulous recipes

▶ www.thisisantwerp.be Antwerp locals present the latest from their city's arts, music, fashion and lifestyle, others leave comments and complement with further tips

APPS

▶ carbu.be Guide to Belgium's cheapest petrol stations, updated daily, very handy

▶ this is antwerp Antwerp's hotspots, for iPhone and Android

▶ ugentpassage Discover Ghent with tips put together by the university

▶ visit-brussels The homepage of the tourist office in Brussels offers several apps helpful in visiting the city

TRAVEL TIPS

ARRIVAL

Access by car: E40 from French ports to Oostende and the coast, Bruges, Ghent and Brussels, or E42 from Dunkirk via Lille to southern Flanders and Brussels. For Antwerp take the E17 from Ghent. Using the motorways is free, only the *Liefkenshoektunnel* of Antwerp's Ring West has a 5.50 euro toll.

The Eurostar train connects London and Brussels several times a day. For other parts of Flanders, change in Bruxelles-Midi to Belgian intercity and regional trains. Those arriving from neighbouring countries will find fast connections several times a day to Brussels or Antwerp from Paris and northern France, the Netherlands, or Cologne and Frankfurt. *Information: www.b-rail.be | www.eurostar.com*

Scheduled flights arrive and depart from Bruxelles-National Aéroport, 15km (9 miles) north-east of the city. Between 5.30am and 0.20am the *Brussels Airport Express* train heads into the city every 15–20 minutes (2nd class 7.60 euros, purchasing the ticket on the train attracts a supplement of 3 euros, journey time 20 minutes). Every hour there are two trains from the airport to Mechelen–Antwerp (2nd class 10.20 euros) and to Leuven (2nd class 7.90 euros). An Airport Express bus leaves from the Brussels train stations every hour to Ghent, and on to De Panne. Travellers headed for Bruges, Oostende, Blankenberge or Knokke change either in Bruxelles-Midi or in Ghent-Sint-Pieters.

Ryanair operates a hub at the Brussels South-Charleroi Airport (50 km/30 miles south of Brussels). From here a shuttle bus to the Bruxelles-Midi train station runs between 8.30am and 11.50pm (13 euros). A TEC bus Ligne A takes travellers to the Charleroi-Sud train station, from where trains run every half hour to Bruxelles-Midi (19.60 euros).

RESPONSIBLE TRAVEL

It doesn't take a lot to be environmentally friendly whilst travelling. Don't just think about your carbon footprint whilst flying to and from your holiday destination but also about how you can protect nature and culture abroad. As a tourist it is especially important to respect nature, look out for local products, cycle instead of driving, save water and much more. If you would like to find out more about eco-tourism please visit: *www.ecotourism.org*

BANKS & MONEY

Opening times Mon–Fri 9am–4pm; in smaller towns, banks often close over lunch. ATMs taking UK credit and debit cards are widespread. Credit cards are accepted nearly everywhere, with Diners Card less common.

CAR

The top speed on Belgian motorways is 120kph, on national roads 90, on Flemish side roads 70, in built-up areas 50, near schools 30 km/h. A seat belt has to be worn on the back seats too. Drink-driving limit: 0.5. Make sure you carry two yellow fluorescent vests in your car. Breakdown assistance: *Touring Wegenhulp | tel. 070 34 47 77 (*)* or *Vlaamse Automobilistenbond VAB | tel. 070 34 46 66 (*)*

CONSULATES & EMBASSIES

UK EMBASSY

Avenue d'Auderghem 10 | Oudergemlaan 10 | tel. 3 22 287 6244 | Mon–Fri 9am–5.30pm | www.ukinbelgium.fco.gov.uk

US EMBASSY

Regentlaan 27 Boulevard du Régent | B-1000 Brussels | tel. 3 22 81 14 000 | Mon–Fri 9am–6pm | www.belgium.usembassy.gov

CUSTOMS

If travelling within the EU, you may import and export goods intended for personal use free of charge. Upper limits only apply to tobacco (800 cigarettes per adult), wine (90 litres) and spirits (10 l). US citizens are subject to much stricter regulations. They may only carry a maximum of 200 cigarettes, 2 litres of alcoholic drinks below 15 per cent and 1 litre of alcohol drinks over 15 per cent.

EMERGENCY

Ambulance, fire service: *tel. 100*
Police: *tel. 101* or *112*

HEALTH

The European Health Service Card (EHIC) is accepted in Belgium. In urgent cases

BUDGETING

Coffee	£ 3 / $ 4.60 *for one cup*
Fries/frites	£ 2.20 / $ 3.30 *for a small portion*
Beer	£ 4 / $ 6 *for a glass of strong beer (0.3l)*
Chocolates	£ 16–85 / $ 25–130 *for 1 kg, depending on the maker*
Petrol	approx. £ 1.50 / $ 2.25 *for one litre*
Taxi	approx. £ 8 / $ 12 *for a short journey (3 km)*

accident & emergency departments (*spoedgevallen,* in Brussels and Wallonia called *urgences*) of the hospitals (white street signs with a red cross and the name of the hospital). Pharmacies (look out for a green neon cross) are usually open 9am–6pm. Night and weekend duty pharmacies (*wacht* or *service de garde*) are advertised in a box at the entrance.

HOSTELS & CAMPING

There are 18 youth hostels in Flanders. Reservations are essential in July and August. In other months book in good time for Antwerp, Bruges and Ghent. *VJH | Van Stralenstraat 40 | B-2060 Antwerp | tel. 03 2 32 72 18 | www.vjh.be*
Information on campsites is available from *www.campings.be.*

TOURISM FLANDERS-BRUSSELS
1a Cavendish Square | London W1G 0LD | tel. 020 7307 7738 | www.visitflanders.co.uk

TOURISM FLANDERS-BRUSSELS
620 Eighth Ave - 44th Floor | New York, NY 10018 | tel. 01 5 84 23 36 | www.visitflanders.us

TOURIST INFORMATION OFFICES IN FLANDERS
www.westtoer.be (Bruges and West Flanders), *www.dekust.org* (coast), *www.toerismeoostvlaanderen.be* (Ghent and East Flanders), *www.vlaamsbrabant.be/toerisme* (Flemish-Brabant), *www.visitbrussels.be* (Brussels), *www.tpa.be* (Antwerp), *www.toerismelimburg.be* (Limburg)

INTERNET & WI-FI

There are plenty of telephone and internet shops near most train stations. Wi-Fi hotspots are available at nearly all railway stations and hotels, as well as in over 500 pubs and restaurants *(www.hierisgratiswifi.be)*. Along the coast, the strip between Knokke-Het Zoute and De Panne is covered, including beaches, campsites and car parks *(costs 4 euros per 30 minutes, 15 euros per day, 25 euros per week, 35 euros for one month | www.citymesh.be)*.

WEATHER IN OOSTENDE

	Jan	Feb	March	April	May	June	July	Aug	Sept	Oct	Nov	Dec
Daytime temperatures in °C/°F	5/41	6/43	9/48	12/54	15/59	18/64	20/68	21/70	19/66	15/59	10/50	7/45
Nighttime temperatures in °C/°F	1/34	1/34	3/37	5/41	8/46	11/52	14/57	14/57	12/54	8/46	5/41	2/36
Sunshine hours/day	2	3	5	7	7	8	7	7	6	4	2	1
Precipitation days/month	14	13	10	10	9	9	12	13	10	14	14	15
Water temperature in °C/°F	7/45	6/43	7/45	8/46	10/50	13/55	15/59	16/61	16/61	14/57	11/52	9/48

Useful internet sites: *www.belgium.be* (general information), *www.flanders.be* (information of the Flemish regional government), *www.resto.be* (restaurant tips), *www.cityplug.be* (information on bars, cafés and clubs), *www.bedandbreakfastflanders.be* (B&Bs), *www.hotels.be* (inexpensive hotel rooms), *www.kkunst.com* (Flemish chansons, pop/rock music), *www.uitinvlaanderen.be* (cultural events), *www.netevents.be* (festivals and parties), *www.sport.be* (sports events), *www.touring.be* (up-to-date traffic information), *www.wegeninfo.be* (information service of the traffic police)

PHONE & MOBILE PHONE

All towns and cities have phone shops. Using a Belgian prepaid card (by Base, Mobistar or Proximus) saves the fees for incoming calls. Calling a landline within Belgium requires dialling the code starting with a 0, followed by the subscriber number (e.g. for Bruges 050 44 46 46). Calling a Belgian mobile phone, first dial the code (from 0475 to 0498) and then the number of the party you want to call. To call Belgium dial the code 0032 for Belgium, then the local code or the mobile phone operator code without the 0, followed by the subscriber number. The dialling code for the UK is 0044, for the US and Canada 001.

In Belgium watch out for numbers starting with 070 or 0900, as they attract supplementary fees that can be hefty.

POST

Letters or postcards to EU countries cost 1.13 euros, to countries outside the EU 1.34 euros. The number of post offices (Mon–Fri 9am–5pm) has been heavily reduced. Stamps are available from many newsagents and stationery shops, as well as from supermarkets, at the *postpunt* or *point poste* (red-and-white sign).

PUBLIC TRANSPORT

Public transport in Flanders is in the hands of a single company, *De Lijn*. Trams run in Antwerp and Ghent, and all resorts on the coast are connected by the *Kusttram (www.dekusttram.be)*. The towns are connected by white-yellow buses. Tickets bought in advance (online, in Lijnwinkel at important stops and at machines): single journey from 1.20 euros (from 2 euros in bus/tram), day pass *(dagpas)* 5 euros, 3-day pass 10 euros, 5-day pass 15 euros (in bus/tram 7 / 12 / 18 euros). In the province of West Flanders there is also a 7-day pass (advance purchase only, 18 euros for 1 person, 30 euros for 2 people). Travellers purchasing tickets in the bus/tram need to have small change ready for the driver (the highest denomination accepted are 10 or 20 euro notes). Individual tickets have to be stamped in the yellow machines at the doors. *www.delijn.be*

Rail travellers are eligible for a 50 per cent discount at weekends, and there are special rates for *excursions.* Young people under 26 years of age are eligible for the good-value *GO-Pass. Information: www.b-rail.be*

WEATHER

Flanders borders the English Channel. The Gulf Stream brings a mild maritime climate. In winter, there is little snow, and you'll get some rain whatever the season. Weather service: *www.meteo.be*

USEFUL PHRASES DUTCH

PRONUNCIATION

To help you with the pronunciation we have added to each word or phrase a simplified guide on how to say it [in square brackets]. Here kh denotes a guttural sound similar to 'ch' in Scottish 'loch', and ü is spoken like 'u' in French 'tu'.

IN BRIEF

Yes/No/Maybe	ja [ya]/nee [nay]/misschien [miss-kheen]
Please/	alstublieft [ashtübleeft]/alsjeblieft
Thank you	[ash-yer-bleeft]/bedankt [bedankt]
Excuse me	Sorry [sorry]
May I ...?/ Pardon?	Mag ik ...? [makh ick]/ Pardon? [spoken as in French]
I would like to .../	Ik wil graag ... [ick vill khraakh]/
Have you got ...?	Heeft u ...? [hayft ü]
How much is ...	Hoeveel kost ...? [hoofayl kost]
I (don't) like that	Dat vind ik (niet) leuk. [dat find ick (niet) lurk]
broken/doesn't work	kapot [kapott]/werkt niet [vairkt neet]
Help!/Attention!/	Hulp! [hülp]/Let op! [lett opp]/
Caution!	Voorzichtig!/[forzikhtikh]
Ambulance	ambulance [ambülantser]
Police/Fire brigade	politie [politsee]/brandweer [brandvayr]

GREETINGS, FAREWELL

Good morning!/afternoon!/	Goeden morgen/dag! [khooyer morkhe/dakh]/
evening!/night!	avond!/nacht! [afond/nakht]
Hello!/goodbye!	Hallo! [hallo]/Dag! [daakh]
See you	Doei! [dooee]
My name is ...	Ik heet ... [ick hayt]
What's your name?	Hoe heet u? [hoo hayt ü]/Hoe heet je? [hoo hayt yer]
I'm from ...	Ik kom uit ... [ick komm owt]

DATE AND TIME

Monday/Tuesday	maandag [maandakh]/dinsdag [dinnsdakh]
Wednesday/Thursday	woensdag [voonsdakh]/donderdag [donderdakh]
Friday/Saturday	vrijdach [fraydakh]/zaterdag [zatterdakh]
Sunday/holiday	zondag [zonndakh]/feestdag [faystdakh]

Spreek jij nederlands?

"Do you speak Dutch?" This guide will help you to say the basic words and phrases in Dutch.

today/tomorrow/ yesterday	vandaag [fanndaakh]/morgen (morkher)/ gisteren (khisteren]
What time is it?	Hoe laat is het? [hoo laat iss hett]
It's three o'clock	Het is drie uur [hett iss dree üür]

TRAVEL

open/closed	open [open]/gesloten [khesloten]
entrance	ingang [innkhang]/inrit [inritt]
exit	uitgang [owtkhang]/*(car park)* uitrit [owtritt], *(motorway)* afslag [affslakh]
departure/ arrival	vertrektijd [fertrekktayt]/vertrek [fertrekk]/ aankomst [aankommst]
toilets women/men	toilet [twalett]/dames [daamers]/heren [hayren]
(not) drinking water	(geen) drinkwater [(kheen) drinkvaater]
Where is ...?/Where are ...?	Waar is ...? [vaar iss]/Waar zijn ...? [vaar zayn]
left/right/ straight ahead/ back/close/far	links [links]/rechts [rekhts]/ rechtdoor [rekhtdor]/ terug [terükh]/dichtbij [dikhtbay]/ver [fair]
bus/tram	bus [büs]/tram [tram]
U-underground / taxi/cab	metro [metro] / taxi [taxi]
bus stop/cab stand	station [stasseeonn]/taxistandplaats [taxistandplaats]
parking lot/ parking garage	parkplaats [parkplaats]/ parkeergarage [parkayrkharager]
train station/harbour	station [stasseeonn]/haven [haafen]
airport	luchthaven [lükhthaafen]
timetable/ticket	dienstregeling [dienstraykheling]/kaartje [kaartyer]
single/return	enkel [enkel]/retour [retour]
train / track/platform	trein [trayn] / spoor [spoor]/perron [peronn]
I would like to rent ...	Ik wil graag ... huren [ick vill khraakh ... hüüren]
a car/a bicycle/a boat	een auto [enn owto]/fiets [feets]/boot [boat]
petrol / gas station	tankstation [tankstasseeonn]
petrol/gas / diesel	benzine [benseen]/diesel [diesel]

FOOD & DRINK

Could you please book a table for tonight for four?	Wilt u alstublieft voor vanavond een tafel voor vier personen voor ons reserveren. [villt ü ashtübleeft for fannaafont en taafel for feer pairzonen for ons reservayren]
on the terrace/ by the window	op het terras [opp het terrass]/ bij het raam [bay het raam]
The menu, please	De kaart, alstublieft. [de kaart ashtübleeft]

Could I please have ...?	Mag ik ...? [makh ick]
bottle/carafe/glass	fles [fless]/karaf [karaff]/glas [khlass]
a knife/a fork/a spoon	mes [mess]/fork [fork]/lepel [laypel]
salt/pepper/sugar	zout [zowt]/peper [payper]/suiker [zowker]
vinegar/oil	azijn [azayn]/olie [olee]
with/without ice/sparkling	met [mett]/zonder ijs [zonder ays]/bubbels [bübbels]
May I have the bill, please?	Mag ik afrekenen [makh ick affraykenen]
bill/receipt	rekening [raykening]/bonnetje [bonnetyer]

SHOPPING

Where can I find...?	Waar vind ik...? [vaar finnt ick]
I'd like .../I'm looking for ...	Ik will ... [ick vill]/Ik zoek ... [ick zook]
pharmacy/chemist	apotheek [apotayk]/drogisterij [drookhisteray]
department store	winkelcentrum [vinkelzentrümm]
supermarket	supermarkt [züpermarkt]
100 grammes/1 kilo	1 ons [onz]/1 kilo [kilo]
expensive/cheap/price	duur [düür]/goedkoop [khootkoap]/prijs [prayss]
more/less	meer [mayr]/minder [minder]

ACCOMMODATION

I have booked a single/ double room	Ik heb een eenpersoonskamer/tweepersoonskamer gereserveerd [ick hepp en aynperzoanskaamer/ tvayperzoanskaamer kghereservayrt]
Do you have any ... left?	Heeft u nog ... [hayft ü nokh]
breakfast/half board	ontbijt [ontbayt]/halfpension [hallfpenseeonn]
full board (American plan)	volpension [follpenseeonn]
at the front/seafront	naar de voorkant/zee [naar de forkannt/zay]
shower/sit-down bath	douche [doosh]/badkamer [battkaamer]
balcony/terrace	balkon [balkonn]/terras [terrass]
key/room card	sleutel [slurtel]/sleutelkaart [slurtelkaart]

BANKS, MONEY & CREDIT CARDS

| bank/ATM | bank [bank]/pinautomat [pinn-owtomaat] |
| cash/credit card | kontant [kontant]/pinpas [pinnpass]/ creditcard [kreditkaart] |

HEALTH

doctor/dentist/ paediatrician	arts [arts]/tandarts [tandarts]/ kinderarts [kinderarts]
hospital/ emergency clinic	ziekenhuis [zeekenhows]/ spoedeisende hulp[spootayzender hülp]
fever/pain	koorts [koorts]/pijn [payn]

diarrhoea/nausea	diaree [diaray]/misselijkheid [misselick-hayt]
inflamed/injured	ontstoken [ontstoaken]/gewond [khevonnt]
pain reliever/tablet	pijnstiller [paynstiller]/tablet [tablett]

POST, TELECOMMUNICATIONS & MEDIA

stamp/letter/	zegel [zaykhel]/brief [breef]/
postcard	aanzichtkaart [aanzikhtkaart]
I need a landline phone card	Ik wil graag een telefoonkaart voor het vaste net. [ick vill khraakh en telephonekaart for het faster net]
I need a prepaid card for my mobile	Ik zoek een prepaid-kaart voor mijn mobieltje. [ick zook en prepaid-kaart for mayn mobeelt-yer]
Where can I find internet access?	Waar krijg ik toegang tot internet [vaar kraykh ick too-khang tot internet]
socket/adapter/ charger	stopcontact [stoppkontakt]/adapter [adapter]/ oplader [oplaader]
computer/battery/ rechargeable battery	computer [computer]/batterij [batteray]/ accu [akkü]
internet connection/wifi	internetverbinding [internetferbinnding]/WLAN
e-mail/file/ print	mail [mail]/bestand [bestant]/ uitdraaien [owtdraa-yen]

LEISURE, SPORTS & BEACH

beach/bathing beach	strand [strand]/strandbad [strandbart]
sunshade/ lounger	zonnescherm [zonner sherm]/ zonnestoel [zonnerstool]
low tide/high tide	laagwater [laakhvaater]/hoogwater [hoakhvaater]

NUMBERS

0	nul [nüll]	15	vijftien [fayfteen]
1	één [ayn]	16	zestien [zesteen]
2	twee [tvay]	17	zeventien [zerventeen]
3	drie [dree]	18	achtien [akhteen]
4	vier [feer]	19	negentien [naykhenteen]
5	vijf [fayf]	70	zeventig [zerventikh]
6	zes [zess]	80	tachtig [takhtikh]
7	zeven [zerven]	90	negentig [naykhentikh]
8	acht [akht]	100	honderd [hondert]
9	negen [naykhen]	200	tweehonderd [tvayhondert]
10	tien [teen]	1000	duizend [dowzent]
11	elf [elf]	2000	tweeduizend [tvaydowzent]
12	twaalf [tvaalf]	10000	tienduizend [teendowzent]
13	dertien [dairteen]	1/2	half [hallf]
14	viertien [feerteen]	1/4	kwart [kvart]

USEFUL PHRASES FRENCH

IN BRIEF

Yes/No/Maybe	oui/non/peut-être
Please/Thank you	s'il vous plaît/merci
Good morning!/afternoon!/ evening!/night!	Bonjour!/Bonjour!/ Bonsoir!/Bonne nuit!
Hello!/goodbye!/See you!	Salut!/Au revoir!/Salut!
Excuse me, please	Pardon!
My name is ...	Je m'appelle ...
I'm from ...	Je suis de ...
May I ...?/ Pardon?	Puis-je ...?/Comment?
I would like to .../ have you got ...?	Je voudrais .../ Avez-vous?
How much is ...?	Combien coûte ...?
I (don't) like this	Ça (ne) me plaît (pas).
good/bad/broken	bon/mauvais/cassé
too much/much/little	trop/beaucoup/peu
all/nothing	tout/rien
Help!/Attention!	Au secours/attention
police/fire brigade/ambulance	police/pompiers/ambulance

TRAVEL

open/closed	ouvert/fermé
entrance/exit	entrée/sortie
departure/arrival	départ/arrivée
toilets/restrooms / ladies/gentlemen	toilettes/femmes/hommes
Where is ...?/Where are ...?	Où est ...?/Où sont ...?
left/right	à gauche/à droite
straight ahead/back	tout droit/en arrière
close/far	près/loin
bus/tram/underground / taxi/cab	bus/tramway/métro/taxi
street map/map	plan de ville/carte routière
train station/harbour/airport	gare/port/aéroport
schedule/ticket	horaire/billet
single/return	aller simple/aller-retour
train/track/platform	train/voie/quai
doctor/dentist/paediatrician	médecin/dentiste/pédiatre
hospital/emergency clinic	hôpital/urgences
internet address (URL)/e-mail address	adresse internet/mail
internet connection/wifi	accès internet/wi-fi

Tu parles français?

"Do you speak French?" This guide will help you to say the basic words and phrases in French.

FOOD & DRINK

The menu, please	La carte, s'il vous plaît.
Could I please have ...?	Puis-je avoir ... s'il vous plaît
bottle/carafe/glass	bouteille/carafe/verre
knife/fork/spoon	couteau/fourchette/cuillère
salt/pepper/sugar	sel/poivre/sucre
vinegar/oil	vinaigre/huile
milk/cream/lemon	lait/crème/citron
with/without ice/sparkling	avec/sans glaçons/gaz
May I have the bill, please	Je voudrais payer, s'il vous plaît
bill	addition

ACCOMMODATION

I have booked a room	J'ai réservé une chambre
single room/double room	chambre simple/double
breakfast	petit déjeuner
half board/	demi-pension/
full board (American plan)	pension complète
shower/sit-down bath	douche/bain
balcony/terrace	balcon /terrasse
key/room card	clé/carte magnétique
luggage/suitcase/bag	bagages/valise/sac

BANKS, MONEY & CREDIT CARDS

bank/ATM/pin code	banque/guichet automatique/code
cash/credit card	comptant/carte de crédit
bill/coin	billet/monnaie

NUMBERS

0	zéro	8	huit
1	un, une	9	neuf
2	deux	10	dix
3	trois	20	vingt
4	quatre	100	cent
5	cinq	1000	mille
6	six	½	un[e] demi[e]
7	sept	¼	un quart

NOTES

FOR YOUR NEXT HOLIDAY ...

MARCO POLO TRAVEL GUIDES

- PACKED WITH INSIDER TIPS
- BEST WALKS AND TOURS
- FULL-COLOUR PULL-OUT MAP
  AND STREET ATLAS

ROAD ATLAS

The green line ▬▬ indicates the Trips & Tours (p. 92–97)
The blue line ▬▬ indicates The perfect route (p. 30–31)

All tours are also marked on the pull-out map

Photo: Brussels, Grand´ Place

125

Zundert
Meerle
Alphen
Hilvaren-beek
Middelb
EINDHOVE
127
17
B
C
35
8

Chaam

Baarle-Nassau
2015
Poppel
Vessem
Bladel-Netersel
Veldh
Hoogstraten
Lage Mierde
Hapert
30
Béguinage
E19
2

Rijkevorsel
Merksplas
Ravels
Reusel
85
A67
N
29
E

Beerse
Turnhout
Arendonk
15
10
Be

West-malle
Oostmalle
15
24
A21
25
26
25

Zoersel
9
22
Retie
Abdij Van Postel
Postel
Lommel

21
19
Dessel
Lille
6
Kasterlee

20
E34
Grobben-donk
Vorselaar
13
Lichtaart
2014
Kempisch Kanaal
e
Mol
14
20
Balen
G

A13
8
6
Herentals
Geel
71
L
m
-E

20
Nijlen
Herent-hout
22
E313
Olen
23
Albert-Kanaal
Meerhout
Leopoldsburg
H

Berlaar
67
Westerlo
12
24
7
25
13
Beringen
Koe

Heist-op-den-Berg
Tongerlo
Abdij-van
14
Tessen-derlo
26
Heu

10
Herselt
Abdij van Averbode
Averbode
20
Paal
26
P
28

19
Rillaar
Aarschot Scherpen-heuvel
29
Diest
Circuit Terlaem

Tremelo
22
E314
23
A2
24
e
25
Lummen
12

Rotselaar
5
Bekkevoort
Tielt
69
Halen
Herk-de-Stad
27
A13

Herent
18
Leuven
(Louvain)
Glabbeek
Kortenaken
29
Hasselt
28

5
106
Lubbeek
Linter
Nieuwerkerken
Zoutleeuw
30
80
Alken
Korte-Wellen

23
10
Butsel
Tienen
(Tirlemont)
Béguinage
St.-Truiden
(St.-Trond)

24
3
E40
Hoegaarden
Orsmaal-Gussen-hoven
Borgloo
Kasteel H

25
Hamme-Mille
25
Landen
Gingelom
Heers

Gréz-Doiceau
26
A3
Jodoigne
Orp-Jauche
130
Hannut
159
Waremme
(Borgworm)

91
Incourt
29
Chaumont-Gistoux
28a
29

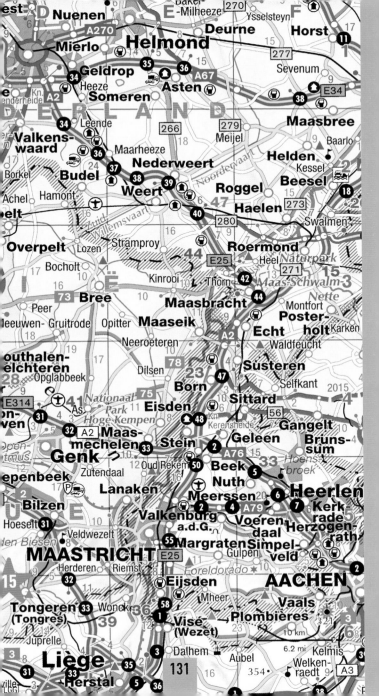

KEY TO ROAD ATLAS

18 — **26**	Autobahn mit Anschlussstellen / Motorway with junctions
	Autobahn in Bau / Motorway under construction
	Mautstelle / Toll station
	Raststätte mit Übernachtung / Roadside restaurant and hotel
	Raststätte / Roadside restaurant
	Tankstelle / Filling-station
	Autobahnähnliche Schnellstraße mit Anschlussstelle / Dual carriage-way with motorway characteristics with junction
	Fernverkehrsstraße / Trunk road
	Durchgangsstraße / Thoroughfare
	Wichtige Hauptstraße / Important main road
	Hauptstraße / Main road
	Nebenstraße / Secondary road
	Eisenbahn / Railway
	Autozug-Terminal / Car-loading terminal
	Zahnradbahn / Mountain railway
	Kabinenschwebebahn / Aerial cableway
	Eisenbahnfähre / Railway ferry
	Autofähre / Car ferry
	Schifffahrtslinie / Shipping route
	Landschaftlich besonders schöne Strecke / Route with beautiful scenery
Alleenstr.	Touristenstraße / Tourist route
XI-V	Wintersperre / Closure in winter
× × × × ×	Straße für Kfz gesperrt / Road closed to motor traffic
8%	Bedeutende Steigungen / Important gradients
	Für Wohnwagen nicht empfehlenswert / Not recommended for caravans
	Für Wohnwagen gesperrt / Closed for caravans
☼	Besonders schöner Ausblick / Important panoramic view

* Wartenstein * Umbalfälle	Sehenswert: Kultur - Natur / Of interest: culture - nature
	Badestrand / Bathing beach
	Nationalpark, Naturpark / National park, nature park
	Sperrgebiet / Prohibited area
	Kirche / Church
	Kloster / Monastery
	Schloss, Burg / Palace, castle
	Moschee / Mosque
	Ruinen / Ruins
	Leuchtturm / Lighthouse
	Turm / Tower
∩	Höhle / Cave
	Ausgrabungsstätte / Archaeological excavation
▲	Jugendherberge / Youth hostel
	Allein stehendes Hotel / Isolated hotel
	Berghütte / Refuge
▲	Campingplatz / Camping site
	Flughafen / Airport
	Regionalflughafen / Regional airport
	Flugplatz / Airfield
	Staatsgrenze / National boundary
	Verwaltungsgrenze / Administrative boundary
⊖	Grenzkontrollstelle / Check-point
⊖	Grenzkontrollstelle mit Beschränkung / Check-point with restrictions
ROMA	Hauptstadt / Capital
VENÉZIA	Verwaltungssitz / Seat of the administration
	Ausflüge & Touren / Trips & Tours
	Perfekte Route / Perfect route
★	MARCO POLO Highlight / MARCO POLO Highlight

INDEX

The index lists all places and destinations mentioned in this guide.
Page numbers in bold refer to the main entry.

WRITE TO US

e-mail: info@marcopologuides.co.uk

Did you have a great holiday?
Is there something on your mind?
Whatever it is, let us know!
Whether you want to praise, alert us
to errors or give us a personal tip –
MARCO POLO would be pleased to
hear from you.
We do everything we can to provide the
very latest information for your trip.

Nevertheless, despite all of our authors'
thorough research, errors can creep in.
MARCO POLO does not accept any
liability for this. Please contact us by
e-mail or post.

MARCO POLO Travel Publishing Ltd
Pinewood, Chineham Business Park
Crockford Lane, Chineham
Basingstoke, Hampshire RG24 8AL
United Kingdom

PICTURE CREDITS
Cover photograph: Bruges, marketplace (Look: age fotostock)
Images: S.-C. Bettinger (1 bottom); DuMont Bildarchiv: Kiedrowski (flap l., 18/19, 47, 75, 79, 96, 102/103), Kluyver
(28, 28/29, 40, 86); R. Freyer (flap r., 52, 60, 63); Glowimages: Robert Harding (White) (36); Huber: Damm
(10/11, 98/99, 133); © iStockphoto.com: Janet Rerecich (16 top), tulcarion (17 bottom); Laif: Gonzalez (9), hemis.
fr (2 centre top, 3 centre, 7, 44, 68/69), Le Figaro Magazine (4); Look: age fotostock (1 top); Madame Moustache
(17 top); Pierre Marcolini: Xavier Harcq (16 centre); mauritius images: Alamy (2 top, 5, 8, 20, 105), ib (Moxter) (3
top, 58/59), ib (gourmet-vision) (26 r.); D. Renckhoff (2 centre bottom, 2 bottom, 3 bottom, 15, 27, 30 bottom,
32/33, 39, 43, 48/49, 57, 67, 81, 82, 88, 92/93, 95, 101, 107, 108 bottom); T. Stankiewicz (29, 34, 50, 55); centre
Thomas (6, 12/13, 30 top, 70, 72, 76, 90, 106/107, 109, 122/123); Toerisme Vlaanderen: De Kievith (106), De
Lausnay (64/65), DVT Mechelen (24/25); Tourism Flanders: Himmer (84/85); Tourism Flanders Brussels: Rufe-
nach (108 top), Westtoer (26 l.); Visit Brussels: J.-P. Remy (16 bottom)

1st Edition 2014
Worldwide Distribution: Marco Polo Travel Publishing Ltd, Pinewood, Chineham Business Park,
Crockford Lane, Basingstoke, Hampshire RG24 8AL, United Kingdom. Email: sales@marcopolouk.com
© MAIRDUMONT GmbH & Co. KG, Ostfildern
Chief editor: Marion Zorn
Author: Sven-Claude Bettinger; Editor: Corinna Walkenhorst
Programme supervision: Ann-Katrin Kutzner, Nikolai Michaelis
Picture editors: Barbara Schmid, Gabriele Forst (Leitung)
What's hot: wunder media, Munich
Cartography road atlas: © MAIRDUMONT, Ostfildern; Cartography pull-out map: © MAIRDUMONT, Ostfildern
Design: milchhof:atelier, Berlin; Front cover, pull-out map cover, page 1: factor product munich
Phrase book in cooperation with Ernst Klett Sprachen GmbH, Stuttgart, Editorial by Pons Wörterbücher
Translated from German by Kathleen Becker, Lisbon; editor of the English edition: John Sykes, Cologne
Prepress: BW-Medien GmbH, Leonberg

DOS & DON'TS

Here are a few tips to avoid any holiday trouble

OVERLOOK THE COASTAL TRAM

The *Kusttram* is a fast means of transport – and a quiet one too. Which is why all crossings are well secured, and the drivers always keep one finger on the horn. Yet again and again accidents happen, some of them horrific. The rules of the road are very clear though: the tram always has the right of way!

DRIVING TOO FAST

Speed limits apply to both locals and visitors, and the Belgian police run strict checks. In Flanders, country roads too are lined with electronic radar devices, and on motorways you increasingly see speed checks installed at regular intervals. Exceeding the limit by 10 km/h costs 50 euros, by 20 km/h as much as 100 euros. Going even faster can cost you your licence as well as the fine. Feel free to work it out yourself on *www.wegcode. be.* The fine has to be paid on the spot – otherwise the car will be confiscated. Flanders is not large, so there is really no need to hurry. In this bike-friendly country, it goes with out saying that drivers should be considerate towards cyclists.

ENDANGERING YOURSELF AND OTHERS AT THE SEASIDE

Holidaymakers on the coast continue to act carelessly – going swimming despite signs banning it, or heading out to sea on a little rubber dinghy. If you get into trouble out of your own doing and have to be fished out of the sea by a *Sea King* rescue helicopters, you will have to pay a hefty 14,245 euros for its deployment – and your life. The Belgian beaches are well signposted with details of which sporting activities are permitted in which zones, whether and when you can take a dog onto the sand, ride a horse, or swim in safety. Be sure to pay attention to this information.

'FORGETTING' YOUR RUBBISH

Leaving your empty can of coke or water bottle by the wayside and dropping a paper tissue or cigarette but can cost you dearly – between 50 and 120 euros depending on where you are.

RELIEVING YOURSELF OUTDOORS

All of a sudden, nature calls, there is no public toilet to be seen anywhere, and the nearest hostelry wants to charge for using their loo. Do pay up, as *wildplassen* is strictly policed, costing 50 euros in Antwerp, 60 euros in Ghent, and in Bruges... 152 euros!